The Wisdom
of Getting Unstuck

MOSAICA PRESS

The Wisdom
of Getting Unstuck

*How to emerge from
and avoid the muddy middle*

Shimshon Meir Frankel

Published by Mosaica Press, Inc.
www.mosaicapress.com
info@mosaicapress.com

In loving memory
of my father and mentor

Charles M. Frankel

שלמה בן שמשון ומלכה ז"ל

Rabbi Yitzchak Berkovits
Sanhedria HaMurchevet 113/27
Jerusalem, Israel 97707
02-5813847

יצחק שמואל הלוי ברקוביץ
ראש רשת הכוללים לינת הצדק
סנהדרייה המורחבת 113/27
ירושלם ת"ו

בס"ד ירושלם ת"ו צרא אפר תשב

Having seen samplings of R' Shimshon Meir

Frankel's new book, *The Wisdom of Getting Unstuck*,

I very much would want to share it with so many

good and talented individuals who are – stuck.

The "syndrome" affects virtually everyone at some point,

but some are there chronically. The book is indeed

filled with wisdom – common sense and beyond, and

offers hope to those who seek it.

May the author find himself having helped

many, and may he continue to serve the tzibbur

with his understanding and Knowledge.

בברכה,

יצחק הלוי ברקוביץ

Table of Contents

SECTION I
The Face of Adversity

SECTION II
Clever or Wise

SECTION III
The Schmutz

SECTION IV

Your Whereabouts

SECTION V

The Daily Grind

SECTION VI

Walk Your Own Path

Acknowledgments

This book has been in the making for some time now. Although extremely enriching, there were moments when the process felt heavy and insurmountable. Due to the guidance of my "betters" and closest confidants, I was *zocheh* to continue moving forward. I wish to show these great givers gratitude for all of the kindness and help that they afforded me along the way. I couldn't have tackled this project without them.

I express my appreciation to my co-researchers, the many people in therapy, *rebbeim*, and practicing psychologists who continue to model and add to the exploration and application of the psychotherapeutic tools and guiding principles garnered from Hashem's holy Torah.

Looking back to my time in university, I thank my professor and mentor, the late Dr. Willard B. Frick, for imparting his mastery of personality development, humanistic psychology, and psychotherapy. He served as associate editor of the *Journal of Humanistic Psychology*, ran a successful practice as a psychotherapist, and was the first to demonstrate to me how one may balance a life between dedication to family, love for one's students, and commitment to one's profession.

I'm grateful to the late Dr. Clark E. Moustakas, who, by being a champion for humanistic and clinical psychology, established the Michigan School of Professional Psychology in Detroit. I learned firsthand from him that emphasizing an "existential-phenomenological" approach allows a practitioner to place full trust in a person's process. This heuristic model encourages people to arrive at their very own positive and insightful therapeutic solutions, which serve them both in therapy and in real life.

I owe a debt of gratitude to the wholesome community of the Kollel Institute of Greater Detroit and thank Rabbi Shmuel Irons for his unwavering unconditional love and soft-spoken guidance.

I thank Rabbi Shimon Shapiro and his family for opening their home to me, embracing me as if family, and joining me in my pursuit toward understanding the deeper life lessons inherent in Hashem's Torah. In the study hall, Rabbi Shapiro enriched our learning with stories and by giving over *pshat* that he had originally gleaned from his Rosh Yeshiva, Rabbi Avigdor Miller. Rabbi Shapiro's description of the thoughtful, clever, and fun-filled outings he would plan with his fourth-grade class always warmed my heart.

My late-night talks with Rabbi Avraham Jacobovitz were invaluable and extremely validating. Before his Rebbetzin would ritually call to remind him to come home at 1:30 in the morning, he would never hesitate to pull a Gemara off the shelf to bring light to our philosophical discussions about the soul, the mind, and the psychology of the heart.

I'm indebted to Dr. Raziel Sobel for our ongoing friendship, his family's continued care and concern for my own, and for modeling what it is to be a true *eved Hashem*. I'm grateful for his elucidation of Rabbi Eliyahu Dessler's *Michtav Me'Eliyahu*, especially at a time when I couldn't access the text on my own, back in the early days of our meetings at Partners in Torah.

I thank Rabbis Menachem Levin and Reuven Millmen for giving me the necessary push and wherewithal to leave Detroit and join the learning community in Eretz Yisrael.

I'm grateful to the late Admor Rabbi Yitzchok Rosenbaum, the Clevelander Rebbe, *zt"l*, for empowering me to "Keep moving forward!" And also to Admor Rabbi Ben-Zion Rabinowicz, the Biala Rebbe, for instructing me: "Keep doing what you're doing!" I imagine their responses were exactly what I deserved for hoping and demanding that they tell me what my direction in life ought to be.

Even though it was the last thing on my mind, I appreciate Rabbi Shulem Borstein, Rosh Yeshiva of Midreshet HaGalil, for offering me a challenging position in his high school as a junior class counselor of Russian Israeli teens. I'm thankful for his *menschlichkeit*, for demonstrating what it means to be a true *melech*, and for pointing me to the healing words that continue to live brightly in King David's book of *Tehillim*.

I'm beholden to Rabbi Yitzchak Dovid Grossman, who through his actions and words taught me how to be *mavdil bein kodesh l'chol*, and how to distinguish between the holy and the profane even during the week. I'm thankful for his lessons in *shalom bayis* and *hachnasas orchim*, and the stories that he told while discussing the photo depicting his father and the late Lelover Rebbe walking arm in arm.

I owe so much to the late Rabbi Nachum Bulman, who, although he was the *mashgiach ruchani* of Ohr Somayach, Jerusalem, advised me to go to Shapell's/Darche Noam, exclaiming, "A normal Litvishe yeshiva will destroy you!"

I'm grateful to Rosh Yeshiva Rabbi Yitzchak Hirshfeld for demonstrating what it means to be a true *eved Hashem*, sharpening my mind through his mentoring, showing me how to learn *Tosafos* like a science, and being the *mesader kiddushin* under my *chuppah*, even when he was steeped in a difficult time of mourning.

Thanks to the Dean of Students, Rabbi Shaya Karlinsky, for embodying and illuminating Shapell's authentic Torah *hashkafah*. He stood in front of the study hall in my first week and declared, "Welcome to reality!" He made it clear that it is Hashem's Torah that truly bonds us. It's the very glue that binds us all together. And when preparing for the world-out-there, he referred me to the plaque sitting prominently on his desk, reading: "Prove to me that I have a problem and that you're the one to solve it."

I'm thankful to Rabbi Eliezer Kwass for his friendship and dating advice, for empowering me to stick to my convictions, and for being the ultimate *shadchan* and *chassan* teacher.

I'm indebted to Rabbi Reuven Kamenetsky for his modesty, his insightful view of the Jewish world, his breadth in Hashem's Torah, and his amazingly clear *pshat* in the Gemara. I'm inspired by Rabbi Kamenetsky's mastery over Rabbi Moshe Chaim Luzzatto's *Mesilas Yesharim*. And, ultimately, I thank him for encouraging me to think for myself.

I appreciate Rabbi Mendel Farber for introducing me to the works of *Maharal*, *Ramchal*, and other *sifrei machshavah*. His stories about his Rosh Yeshiva, Rabbi Yitzchok Hutner, are timeless. I thank him for pushing me to think on my own and uplifting me with his indelible words: "Shimshon Meir, if it's the last thing I do, I'm going to pull you up by your bootstraps."

I'm thankful to my Rosh Kollel, Rabbi Shuki Reich, and his hardline approach to learning and test-taking. Due to his mentorship, I fell in love with the words of the *Arbaah Turim* and the *Beis Yosef*. Due to his encouragement, I was able to master the art of composing tables and charts and to feel competent and confident in my learning. If not for his attention to detail and his close relationship with Rabbi Zalman Nechemia Goldberg, I probably wouldn't have *semichah* today.

I owe much to my Rosh Yeshiva, Rabbi Chaim Brovender, for his mentorship, always keeping things simple, his vital insights into human emotion and behavior, and for demonstrating how every problem in life is pedagogical. And thanks to his trust in the power of Hashem's Torah to transform people for the better, I very much appreciate the time he allowed me to just sit and learn. I will always be grateful that he appointed me as "counselor" of the yeshiva. It was the most uplifting job I've ever had.

I appreciate Rabbi Dovid Fink for keeping Hashem's Torah fresh and sharp in the world, his devotion to maintaining the basics, and for making sure that my family stays on the halachic straight and narrow.

A big thanks to my writing coach and editor, Mrs. Alisa Brooks, for helping me get this project off the ground. That's huge! I'm impressed with her professionalism, and I'm grateful for her patience, support, and guidance. I'm particularly thankful for her validation throughout my lengthy brainstorming period, and ultimately for her being a positive advocate from the time I sculpted an initial outline until I arrived at a final first draft.

A big shout-out to Rebbetzin Dena Udren for voluntarily reading through the first draft of the manuscript. I truly hope she is pleased with some of the changes I made due to her helpful comments and suggestions.

Thanks to Rabbi Mati Friedman for his relentless determination. And to Rabbi Yitzchak Berkovits for taking the time in his extraordinarily busy schedule to consider my manuscript and write such a positive letter of endorsement.

I value the entire team at Mosaica Press for their professionalism, experience, creativity, design acumen, and serious attention to detail. I've been honored by Rabbi Yaacov Haber's involvement from the start, and had he not been so enthusiastic about doing a project together, I don't think I would have truly made my mark.

I thank my editor, Rabbi Doron Kornbluth, for his patience, professionalism, sharp eye and analysis, joy in playing the devil's advocate, and for making my first experience with publishing enjoyable, inspiring, and memorable. After reading his (mostly negative) initial comments, he empowered me with his epic proclamation, "Your book is good, but with a little work, it can be great!"

I'm thankful for the unique fortune to have had a father and mentor, the late Mr. Charles M. Frankel, who never hesitated to unearth for me the hidden mysteries of the world. He showed me love, taught me the formula for understanding humanity's greatest struggles, revealed the secrets to developing and maintaining a successful marriage, and modeled what it takes to be a truly good friend. His words continue to live on in my heart, the hearts of others, and also in this book.

Having two parents to guide me both emotionally and psychologically has been a significant privilege. I'm grateful to my mother, Mrs. Lora L. Frankel, for her love and continued support. I cherish the talks we had and the guidance I received from her throughout the writing process, and which I continue to receive. My mother has always given me sound advice. It was she who informed me as a young child: "You need to work on your relationship with G-d." I've been devoted to that pursuit ever since.

I very much appreciate my in-laws, Charles and Diane Radin, for providing a solid home imbued with strong Jewish/family values, and for being such good examples as parents. They have always placed great emphasis on education and the importance of lifelong learning. Their constant support and determination to maintain a relationship with their many grandchildren despite being many miles away are commendable.

I'm grateful to Hashem for our ongoing relationship, His Torah, my *chelek*, walking me through each step of this project, and honoring me with an amazing family, good friends, and the wisest of teachers. I'm also thankful for having been granted such a meaningful and significant profession. I hold dear to my heart every moving and insightful conversation that Hashem and I have had along the way.

I want to thank my wife, Faigel Tziporah, my *eishes chayil*, the *mechaneches* and mother of our children, my best friend, skilled copy editor and parenting teacher, who—for the sake of our *shalom bayis*—avoided getting involved in this writing project altogether.

I'm grateful to my children, Leah Malka, Esther, Devorah, Shmuel Chaim, Miriam, and Gavriel, for their love and acceptance. Their patience has been notably tried by the many late nights I was tucked away in my office, writing to my heart's content.

Last but not least, I would also like to thank—and I'm sure they meant well—the psychologists, rabbis, authority figures, and negative voices in my head that managed to steer me in the wrong direction. In retrospect, I wouldn't have accomplished this project without them.

My muddy mistakes have lent me greater resilience, fortitude, and strength of character. They've also helped me to gather some very important information along my way. One thing I've learned for certain is that there are times when it behooves us not to be bashful in the face of adversity.

Shimshon Meir Frankel

Tammuz 5780

Introduction

I get stuck.

I'm feeling pretty muddled right now. I've arrived at an impasse. I'm at an in-between stage with the writing of this book, and I must admit, it's thoroughly captivating. I recently received a big content edit (filled with useful comments), and I'm racking my brain trying to figure out how to redraft a new and compelling introduction.

And here I am, again, unsure of what to say. I'm feeling anxious, a bit nervous. I'm unclear what my next step should be. When I don't exactly know where I'm headed, my self-confidence starts to wane. It's a really uncomfortable place to be. When I'm tangled in this mess, it always amazes me that there are people who have actually learned to embrace and find joy in this part of the process.

I can't help but remember the first time I felt equally as befuddled. I had just departed from my meeting with the staff at Mosaica Press. The discussion went well. My twenty-minute presentation was received with positivity, enthusiasm, encouragement, and warm smiles. And although they referred to their staff as a "team," I left feeling like they were more like family.

I was truly stoked to start writing. But like any other beginning, I was filled with both excitement and trepidation. I was hesitant to take my first step forward. I found solace in the fact that I wouldn't be starting the project from scratch. I had a document filled with useful information floating somewhere in the cloud. It was a series of lectures I had recorded and transcribed just a year earlier.

I peered outside the window of the train, and that's when it dawned on me. I was struck by an anxious thought: *But now I have to write a book! How does one turn a series of lectures into a book?* Feelings of dread filled my body. I looked outside of myself as if to find the answer, but my thoughts were too muddied to see one. I was in a funk. I hadn't even begun the project and somehow had already succeeded to lose track of who I was in the process.

In truth, I may have felt stuck, but I wasn't really lost. I knew my exact whereabouts. I was wading knee-deep in a very familiar location. It was a place I'd visited many times before and had become accustomed to call *"the muddy middle."*

> *See the piggy*
> *See the puddle,*
> *See the muddy little puddle.*
> *See the piggy in the middle*
> *Of the muddy little puddle.*
> *See her dawdle, see her diddle*
> *In the muddy, muddy middle.*
> *See her waddle, plump and little,*
> *In the very merry middle.*[1]

If you haven't guessed already, these words are found in the introduction to a children's book, *The Piggy in the Puddle.* The story depicts a family standing around a "muddy little puddle." In the middle of the puddle is a little piggy, and her fuddy-duddy parents (and brother) are trying to convince her that it's in her best interests to remove herself from its sticky influence. She is way too happy frolicking about in its muddy, muddy middle to pay heed to their warnings. In order to reprimand her and coax her out, her family members wave a bar of soap in

---

1. Charlotte Pomerantz, *The Piggy in the Puddle* (Macmillan, 1974).

front of her. Unswayed by this intervention, she responds by saying, "Oofy-poofy, oofy-poofy—NOPE!"

The contents of any good book are meant to send a particular message, and while doing so, they often reflect life's many trials and tribulations. What I didn't realize was how much the writing process itself mirrors the struggles of normal everyday life. And for authors, writing is their life. It's what consumes most of their thoughts and time. I might have first heard the words ringing in a children's book, but how apropos it was to have stumbled upon such a fitting literary term. By Divine "coincidence," I had also fallen into what other writers refer to as the "muddy middle."

There are many stages to the writing process, and just like in real life, it's not unusual for an author to begin feeling uneasy somewhere along the way. For example, Rohan Maitzen, a passionate English professor, writer, and blogger, may have a lot of writing experience under her belt but claims that the "in between" stage still continues to offer her "so much uncertainty."

It doesn't just slow her down in the middle; it tends to exhaust her efforts at various points along the way. Maitzen reports, "I still find the phase of writing in between the taking-notes-and-doing-pre-writing stage and the producing-a-reasonably-decent-draft stage psychologically taxing."

When Maitzen is caught in the muddy middle, she gets jumbled up and confused. It's difficult for her to see beyond the chaos, as she describes, "The words are all in a kind of virtual heap and I can't yet see what order to put them in, or how to choose among them, or how to say them properly (clearly, eloquently)."[2]

However unclear and uncomfortable it may be, with ample experience, Maitzen has become wiser to these murky times, stating, "I'm learning to trust my own process more: I know from experience that this muddy middle is a phase of its own." Believing in the process has helped her to anticipate and become more confident about what

2.   Rohan Maitzen, "The Muddy, Muddy Middle: My Writing Process."

may happen in the future, saying, "Eventually, though, I know I will get out of the mess...I can almost see now, too, how the parts will fit together—almost!" In the darkest of times, she has developed the confidence, trusting "that the next phase will come."

The path to completion is never an easy one. When sculpting her children's books, Nikki Tate talks about the difficulties that often arise. She's a prolific writer and, much like Maitzen, has managed to become wary of the many pitfalls. She's learned that at a particular point in the writing process, she will inevitably fall into a rut and lose clarity. "There's a stage in every writing project where the first draft seems unfinishable," she says. Due to experience, she knows that the fuzziness will begin to surface around the "fifty–seventy-five percent mark...By then, I'm frustrated by how slow things are going, feel like I'm never going to finish the first draft," she reports.

Being wise to this mark has its benefits. Over time, Tate has learned to find joy and excitement in the buildup: "But just before I get to that dreadful muddy middle where it seems there is no realistic chance I will ever finish writing the first draft, there's a lovely stage of enthusiasm and ease that lasts up until the first third is done."[3]

I find comfort in Amanda Rawson Hill's simple definition of the muddy middle. While writing her novel she blogged about her process, describing the muddy middle as that place where "you're stuck and not sure how to get from point A to point B."[4] It's reassuring to learn that none of us are alone when it comes to stumbling into the muck. We all know what it's like to lose direction in life at one point or another.

Joe Moore, a novelist and writer of children's books, had just reread *Gone with the Wind* and recounted how much of the script reflects the difficulties of normal everyday life. The book contains sixty-three chapters, and he considers the first five as an introduction. He cheekily asks, "So what did Margaret Mitchell fill the fifty-seven chapters in between with? Challenges, obstacles, reversals of fortune for characters." Let's be honest. We find excitement in the turbulence of life. We may not

---

3.   Nikki Tate, "Repost: Just Before the Muddy Middle."
4.   Amanda Rawson Hill, "Surviving the Muddy Middle."

always be conscious of it, but much of life takes place smack-dab in the muddy middle.[5]

A nonfiction writer's job is to capture and relate to the reader a taste of real life. And imagine how much of a kinship we may feel with an author who is willing to share her own struggles.

Let's take a look at another example. There's nothing that tugs at a mother's heart more than a sick child. How difficult it must be when no one can figure out what's actually ailing him. It can be a very troubling and dark place to be, especially when the medical tests continue to show inconclusive results.

While waiting for her son's diagnosis, Lynnette Shepherd, a parenting coach and blogger, related what it was like to live inside this murky process: "Here I sit in the muddy middle, where nothing is clear, and there are more questions than answers. Each time we think we might be moving, another roadblock appears to delay the process."

How many medical reviews and committees can a mother possibly sit through?

At the time, Shepherd felt like her life was being held together by just a thread. As time passed, she had an epiphany of sorts and merited to develop a new outlook: "As much as I want answers, a diagnosis, and timelines so I can wrap my mind around whatever comes next, I'm growing to appreciate the muddy middle."

Although it hadn't been easy, Shepherd indicated that she finally learned the "value of the muddy middle." She saw it as an opportunity to place the fate of the medical process in the hands of Hashem. It was her trust in Hashem that would keep up her spirits. With His help, she'd be able to avoid being swallowed up by the "murky depths," and ultimately, strengthen the thread that had been holding her life together all along.[6]

I'm impressed at what we can glean from the experience of the authors I quoted above. Whatever path we're taking in life, we're all bound to get stuck at some point along the way. It's not always clear how to move

---

5.   Joe Moore, "The Muddy Middle: Where Good Plots Go to Die."
6.   Lynette Sheppard, "Learning to Appreciate the Muddy Middle."

from point A to point B. Yet, there's hope. Every time we pull ourselves out of the muck, we become wiser and more confident.

As I write this, in order to move further, I bring to mind the many times I've succeeded at schlepping my legs out from the muckiness. And although there's an option to wallow in its "very merry middle," I'm starting to see this part of the journey as an opportunity to write my story in my own way. I'm learning to embrace life with the press of every key, and with Hashem's help, trust the process as I continue to progress forward.

THIS BOOK HAS PURPOSE

This book is for people who are interested in regaining control of their lives. It contains clever ways to set aside the concerns that hold us back from moving forward.

Walking yourself through this book will make you feel like you're controlling the shots. And you'll be able to set yourself free from the foreign thoughts and unhealthy behaviors that have been keeping who you truly are at bay.

In the following chapters, you'll learn how to listen (and speak) to your soul, identify the bad spots, focus on your good parts, live according to your true values, and tell your story in the way you've always yearned to have it told.

The tools and guiding principles in this book possess great potential to transform peoples' lives for the better. If it helps you to move one step closer toward becoming the best version of yourself, I'll be able to confidently say that I have, thankfully, done my small part.

The Face of Adversity

Chapter 1

Your Antagonist

Y ou are the author of your own story. You're the main character and, as you know, a compelling story always has the main character come into conflict with an opposing force.

This force is your *Antagonist*.

It wants to see you struggle. It snuggles up next to you, rubs its shoulders against you, and attempts to feed you its lines all day long. It wants you to follow its script, not yours. The Antagonist tries to distort our vision. It blurs the lenses with which we view ourselves and the world around us. Our perception of reality becomes muddied by its foreign messages and external expectations. It's easy to become misguided by its thick layers of deception.

Would you describe yourself as a wise person? You've got your struggles just like everyone else. You're most likely wiser in some aspects of your life than others, and whether you're fully aware of it or not, you're always making efforts to become the person you truly want to be.

Have you ever met anyone who isn't grappling with something? We're all struggling with one thing or another. Every one of us has an Antagonist.

The Antagonist leaves us good reason to be concerned. It does everything in its power to distract us and entice us into doing the wrong thing. When we start to identify ourselves with the negative messages that it delivers, we're bound to start experiencing a heightened degree of discomfort, emptiness, pain, and tension.

Chapter 2

It's a Bother

Y ou've probably already given what's bothering you a name, whether lonely, confused, doubtful, scared, anxious, down, or lacking impulse control. When those feelings hit, we may not immediately know where they came from. In order to get a better grasp on what we are experiencing, like good diagnosticians, we tend to break down our negative behaviors and thought patterns into simple terms. We can learn a lot from the labels that we place upon ourselves. The real problem arises when we start to define ourselves by them. Once we start basing our most important life decisions on our Antagonist's ill-driven directives, that's when we know we've stumbled right into the muddy middle.

Imagine making life decisions based on your own values, making choices that look right and feel good, and whenever you decide to take your next step, you can count on it to be firmly planted and well secured. What if you could establish a mutual understanding with your Antagonist and change the relationship for the better? Nothing could stop you from writing your own story in your own way. You'd have the freedom to develop a narrative that suits you best.

In order to start relating to our Antagonist on our own terms, we have to become wiser to its daily shenanigans. As long as we're convinced of its rhetoric, however, it will continue to rule over us and dictate our lives.

It takes a wise person to be able to avoid their Antagonist's whims, but when we time and time again find ourselves stuck in the muddy middle, it's upon us to start developing new and clever ways to finagle ourselves out from the middle of its sticky mud.

TAKEAWAYS

- Your Antagonist is an opposing force. It distorts your vision, blurring the lenses of how you view yourself and the world around you.
- Basing your life's decisions on the labels (i.e., anxious, depressed, addicted) that you place upon yourself propels you right into the muddy middle.
- It's wise to understand your Antagonist's ways, or it will continue to rule over you.
- When you're living according to your own values, you're free to walk your own path.

Clever or Wise

The dean of students approached the podium at the front of the study hall. He moved his eyes around the room and asked the students, "Do you know the difference between the clever person and the wise person?"

The room was silent. It was obviously a rhetorical question. The dean quickly responded to his own question by stating: "The clever person is cunning enough to get out of any sticky situation in which he finds himself. The wise person is smart enough to have not gotten himself stuck into the situation in the first place."

These concepts are well elucidated in one of the early compilations of Jewish Law. The first volume of the Arbaah Turim (Tur) discusses the laws for daily practice. It focuses on what we do as we roll out of bed in the morning, highlights the activities that we perform throughout the day, and concludes with what we do as we crawl back into bed at night.

How would you introduce this body of daily law and practice? Surprisingly, the volume begins with a Mishnah from Pirkei Avos (Ethics of Our Fathers). According to the Rambam, the main concern of Pirkei Avos is to teach us about the lofty character traits and deep wisdom inherent in the Jewish Sages and, even more significantly, to demonstrate for us how to live by their example (Rambam, Pirkei Avos, Mishnah 1).

Why does the Tur begin with an "ethical tract"? Knowing that we hardly ever enact laws from a Mishnah, we may assume that this section comes to serve a different purpose (Sotah 22a). From its placement at the beginning, we may deduce that developing and refining ourselves are prerequisites to learning the laws which govern our daily practices.

Yehudah Ben Teima says:
Be strong as a leopard,
light as an eagle,
swift as a deer,
and mighty as a lion
to do the will of your Father in Heaven.

(Pirkei Avos 5:20)

Chapter 3

The Wise Person: Yehudah ben Teima

THE EAGLE

The *Tur* clarifies Yehudah ben Teima's teaching. He explains that being light as an eagle is equated to seeing with our eyes. The eagle floats in the air. It soars among the clouds and gazes at everything below from a bird's-eye view. The eagle has keen vision from above, allowing it to be critical of what lies ahead. Like the eagle, wise people see everything and know when to avert their eyes to avoid focusing on the things that might affect them negatively.

Gazing upon that which is not in our best interest brings with it the risk of us seeing that which may capture us in its grasp, and cause us to fall away from our path, losing sight of ourselves. We'll miss the mark, fall off-step, trip, and quickly stumble into the quagmire. It's a simple theorem: your eyes see, your heart desires, and you finish the deed. It only takes a split second to find oneself sliding down the wrong path.

A bird's-eye view gives us the ability to shift our sights, change our focus, and point ourselves in the right direction. The eagle eye is very acute. It has the uncanny ability to change its focus from an entire valley to a scope of ten square inches—from a thousand yards away. We, too, can zero in on what suits us best. Soaring above allows us to perceive the greater picture. Having a bird's-eye view offers proper perspective. It allows us to recognize the dangerous parts, stay on top of things, and maintain a proper trajectory as we continue to walk along our path.

Our eyes are highly impressionable. In order to not be thrown off-kilter, wise people shield their eyes from negative external influences. When we let down our guard, even for a brief moment, foreign messages and expectations are allowed to slip through our lenses, clouding the windows to our soul. The real issue arises when we begin defining ourselves by such rhetoric. Listening to our Antagonist's unhealthy notions leads us to doubt and feel distant from ourselves. These messages become so ingrained in us that the voice that echoes in our mind starts to sound like our very own. Some of its narratives may be recently adopted, but others we've been carrying around since childhood. We've all heard messages like:

- "Why can't you learn as well as Benny?"
- "You're the most talented in your class."
- "Why are you so lazy?"
- "You're the smartest in your grade."
- "How come you never smile?"
- "Your sister is the creative one in the family."
- "You're not good enough to play."
- "Eat! You need to put some meat on those bones."
- "You're the pretty one in the family."
- "Stop with the pastries. It's not like you've got your sister's figure."

Although our parents, friends, teachers, and other authority figures might have meant well, some of the stories and labels they have projected upon us are far from empowering. Many old messages, shared with the greatest of intentions, have been received as highly negative. Even though praise for one's natural talents and good looks may appear positive on the surface, it is only a trap. The message is negative and also tends to breed an unhealthy view of oneself. Such praise is bad not just because it teaches us to compare ourselves to others, but it also encourages us to focus on the things in life that we truly have no control over. Only our individual efforts should be applauded. The work and sweat that we put into life is what should be celebrated and rewarded.

If you're viewing yourself through external eyes, you're most likely basing your life's choices on these foreign perceptions, an outside-in approach. When left unprotected, we risk exposing our most intimate, sacred space. A wise person doesn't offer an open invitation to the grubby hands of negative outside influences.

Knowing how impressionable we can be, Yehudah ben Teima demands that we take action, that we close our eyes to the negative ideas and foreign expectations that we encounter every day. This way we can keep our sights directed inward and focus on the person we truly want to be. The eagle eye is discerning and gives us a clear perspective. This is how a wise person chooses to walk through life. The approach is a proactive one and is exactly what we need to successfully interact with our world from the inside-out.

THE LION

According to the *Tur*, Yehudah ben Teima's Mishnah is coming to teach that our heart corresponds to the attributes of a lion.[1] In other words, we should approach our life's work as would a mighty lion. In order to stick close to our path, we need to be courageous, and that requires a firmness of purpose.

Living according to our own story is a job fit only for the lionhearted. It is in the chambers of our heart where we find the courage to make proper, healthy, and educated life decisions. Our heart is home to inspiration, and the space in which we can freely choose to walk down either a good path or a bad one. In challenging times, the wisdom in our heart encourages us to take pause and reflect, reorient, and redirect. In the face of our Antagonist's alternative plans, it's always wise to have our best interests at heart.

A lion is inwardly mighty and outwardly inspirational. It is a wise leader—it is King of the Jungle! It is proactive, intuitively working

---

1.   *Tur, Orach Chaim* 1:1.

from the inside-out. The lionhearted don't need to draw attention to themselves through externalities. They already know who they are. They know their purpose.

Yehudah ben Teima believes that you can strengthen and protect yourself and avoid letting every little thing in life throw you off course.

The Sages teach us that the symbol of Yehudah is the lion. Jews are called *Yehudim*, which is an empowering label that reminds us that we're intrinsically mighty. Just as the young Yehudah was appointed by Yaakov, who blessed him, saying, "You are a lion's cub,"[2] we have all been designated to be leaders.

A simple swapping of the letters in the word *aryeh*, lion, transforms the letters into the word *yirah*, awe. A Jew's awe of Hashem lives deep within the heart. It is an internal, intimate, and ongoing relationship.

Allowing foreign messages and external expectations to slip through our eyes ignites an insatiable desire. Once our hearts are swayed in their direction, it's already too late, and our legs will sprint to the finish. But Yehudah ben Teima has great faith in us. He believes that even if we falter with our eyes, we still have the power to take charge. He is confident that we own the insight to take pause and to question any rush of desire. As wise people, we have the means to stop the negative flow by guiding ourselves from deep within our hearts.

We are able to catch ourselves en route and personally inquire: *Is this yearning really a good thing for me? Is pursuing this feeling really in my best interest?* Our eyes will always be bombarded by unhealthy external influences, but with plenty of experience, in unclear and muddy times, we will be able to gather enough strength in our hearts to direct our eyes away from any sight of trouble.

Our hearts' authentic desire will call out to us, roaring, "Protect yourselves! Ignore the bad messages and misleading images that continue to pop up before you." But we'll still make mistakes, and there's also purpose to that.

---

2. *Bereishis* 49:9.

Over time, we become wiser to the misleading messages that seek to lead us astray, and we'll see them for what they truly are.

When we put our full heart into life, along with a been-there-done-that attitude, we are better able to return to the drawing board and redraft our personal narratives for the better. Then we can confidently adjust our sights and start walking in the right direction.

THE DEER

Our legs are likened to the quickness of a deer. They're built for speed, and their ultimate purpose is to help us run to do good. Legs mean action, and they're the very tools that lead us out of life's many hazardous situations.

The *Tur* cautions about how easy it is to fall prey to the negative influences that often seep into our heart. If we're not careful with our eyes at the start, our legs will surely run to the finish. It's like driving in a nail—it leaves us with a sense of permanence. We wind up feeling stuck, disconnected, disoriented, and distant from the person we truly want to be. Although we couldn't be any closer to who we actually are, the illusion is quite convincing, and unfortunately, many of us end up wallowing in our mistakes. Feelings of doubt, blame, and ineptitude are demoralizing.

How do we find our way out? When we grow tired of feeling stuck, we can always get inspired by moving our legs. When we're at risk of losing ourselves in the muddy middle, it's a propitious time to get moving like a deer. When encountering a predator, our legs run away instinctively. Similarly, when we're stuck, we can leave the scene—both physically and figuratively. Once our legs are moving, our heart is ignited, directing us to solid ground.

Once we start feeling more secure, we can then set our sights on what we really care about. Focusing on what we truly value is always an invitation to approach life from the inside-out.

When we find ourselves feeling down, anxious, or caught like the proverbial "deer in the headlights," our legs will be our best resource. A change of scenery usually does the trick. It may be just enough to take in a deep breath and imagine ourselves breathing in a more secure place.

Once we're able to picture ourselves in a new light and see ourselves from a new angle, it's much easier to refresh our view on life.

According to the *Tur*, Yehudah ben Teima is revealing that our legs are built for doing acts of kindness both for ourselves and others. Each step we take toward good creates another channel for good. Putting our legs into motion invites more good into our lives and into the lives of others.

Removing ourselves from the muddy middle is, in itself, an act of kindness.

THE LEOPARD

Being bold as a leopard is known to be synonymous with extreme brazenness and stubbornness. Although Yehudah ben Teima strategically lists this trait at the beginning of his Mishnah, I've chosen to discuss it last in order to stress its considerable importance. According to the *Tur*, this fundamental attribute takes precedence over all the others.

In order for a wise person to develop a critical eye of what lies before them, they must first be shameless in the face of negative outside forces.

It's alarming that Yehudah ben Teima would even present this trait in his Mishnah. The Sages teach us that being brazen, or *azus panim* (lit., "boldness of face"), should be avoided at any cost. Boldness, *azus*, is considered a highly unfavorable personality trait. It is characterized by hardness, shamelessness, and a lack of restraint or regard for another's feelings. Rabbi Yehudah HaNasi was even known to begin his personal morning prayers by beseeching: "May it be Your will, Hashem, my G-d, and G-d of my forefathers, that You rescue me today from brazen people (*azei panim*) and from [my own] brazenness (*azus panim*)."[3] Those who established our morning prayers saw fit to include this paragraph for everyone to recite.

All the more surprising, Yehudah ben Teima seems to contradict himself by continuing his very Mishnah with the following: "The brazen person (*az panim*) heads to the purgatory of Gehinnom, whereas one who is shamefaced (*bosh panim*) will enjoy Gan Eden."[4]

---

3. *Berachos* 16b.
4. *Pirkei Avos* 5:20.

Is brazenness good or bad?

There is a season for everything. Every attribute can be used either for the good or for the bad. In the beginning of his Mishnah, Yehudah ben Teima is emphasizing that there is a positive side to being brazen, and it is wise to implement it when necessary.

> *Who is like the wise person, and who knows the meaning of a thing? A person's wisdom makes his face shine, and the boldness of his face is transformed.*[5]

A wise person has a strong constitution and holds a positive self-regard. Being bold as a leopard may be mistakenly viewed as arrogance, but being "hard" and unbending sometimes has its place: when we encounter negative outside influences, it can be detrimental to be bashful. It's essential to be bold in the face of doubt and to deflect alien messages and outside expectations.

The *Tur* indicates that there will be times in our lives when we will be presented with the right thing to do. And when we want to do this right thing, there'll be an upsurge of energy—a negative force—that will pop up and try to distract us from accomplishing our goals.

On the surface, the *Tur* blames this force on the people we encounter in daily life, but it truly goes deeper. Our Antagonist has actually become clever enough to speak to us in our own language. It's mastered our tone of voice, our every intonation. Its grandiloquence tries to throw us off track and make it nearly impossible for us to do the right thing—and we require a good pair of blinders to keep out all its noise.

The leopard is a solitary and territorial animal. It is not even intimidated by animals that outweigh it. We, too, can choose not to be intimidated by such opposing forces. Yehudah ben Teima believes that we can be unabashed in the face of adversity.

Are we living up to the expectations of Yehudah ben Teima? Are we thinking and acting wisely? It takes a wise person to avoid getting stuck in our Antagonist's muddy meddling.

---

5. *Koheles* 8:1.

TAKEAWAYS

Yehudah ben Teima implores us to be "strong as a leopard, light as an eagle, swift as a deer, and mighty as a lion to do the will of your Father in Heaven."

The Eagle

- Seeing things from above, from a bird's-eye view, allows us to avoid negativity, gives us perspective, and helps us to maintain the proper trajectory.
- Looking at the wrong thing causes us to lose sight of ourselves, but an eagle eye allows us to zero in on what suits us best.

The Lion

- The heart is home to inspiration, and it is from there that we choose to walk down either a good path or a bad one.
- Mistakes make us wiser to the ways of our desires, lending us the wherewithal to catch ourselves en route, question any rush of desire, and take charge.

The Deer

- Legs mean action, and they are built to do good and invite good into our lives and into the lives of others.
- When stuck in a sticky situation, it is our legs that get us moving, enabling us to leave the negative influences behind.

The Leopard

- A wise person has a strong constitution and holds a positive self-regard.
- A leopard is solitary and unintimidated. In order to avoid stumbling into the muddy middle, we must wear blinders and be unabashed in the face of negative outside forces.

Chapter 4

The Clever Person: King David

Alittle over a thousand years before Yehudah ben Teima's Mishnah came into circulation, King David was also inclined to focus on his eyes, heart, and legs. But as the *Tur* points out, in order to tell his own story, he took a reverse approach:

- King David first focused on his legs and beseeched Hashem, "Lead me on the path of Your statutes [Your ways], for that is my desire."
- He then entreated, "Turn my heart toward Your testimonies [Your Torah] and not to greed."
- Last, he requested, "Avert my eyes from seeing falsehood; with Your ways sustain me."[1]

The role of a wise person has been wonderfully elucidated by Yehudah ben Teima. What does the King of Israel achieve by reversing the order of things? By first focusing on the legs, King David illuminates the path of the *clever person*. In other words, if we weren't wise enough to avoid the uncomfortable situation into which we've stumbled, we're going to require a very tactical and quick getaway.

---

1. *Tehillim* 119:35–37.

King David's personal journey testifies to how we may strategically overcome life's stickiest situations. He draws from his own life experiences to adeptly guide us through the many pitfalls we're bound to encounter along our way. He believes that we, too, can soar to the great heights of Yehudah ben Teima; but for King David, the path toward becoming a wise person is a clever one.

Remember how impressionable our eyes can be? According to the *Tur*, we can't afford to rely on the notion that only good things will be delivered before our eyes. We need to take special care to protect our eyes from the common trappings—the eye candy that bombards us, whether in the streets or in the media.

How many times has this scenario happened to you? You're walking down the sidewalk minding your own business, and you turn the corner, and blamo! A terribly eye-catching, mesmerizing, and not-so-healthy-thing-for-you is staring you right in the face.

You're already looking in its direction.

It's simply unavoidable.

Life is full of surprises, and it takes a lot of technical know-how to be able to redirect our eyes at a moment's notice. We're all destined to fall under the spell of our gaze, so before we embark on our journey, like King David, we must first pray for no surprise attacks along the way. There's enough to grapple with in life without us also having to worry about what might be waiting to pounce on us around the corner.

King David had a lot of experience finding himself in difficult situations. His eyes would often become entangled in the honeytrap and his legs would quickly tumble into the sticky muck.

His book of *Tehillim* speaks volumes of his personal struggles. His poetic words affirm the many intimate trials and tribulations he was able to overcome in his life. Through his personal narrative, he masterfully imparts his clever method for freeing oneself of unhealthy desires, negative external influences, and self-evading pursuits.

Just like King David, when caught in the middle of predicament, we may not even remember how we arrived. Life is very blurry in the muddy, muddy middle.

YOUR ONLY RECOURSE

What's your recourse?

Maybe thinking deeply about our actions would work. But if we were of sound mind, how could we have allowed ourselves to be manipulated into our current state in the first place? Can we really regain control of our thoughts right now? Our heart chose its desired path, it flowed with excitement, and now we're standing muddled, knee-deep in the muddy middle.

Our best option is to encourage our legs to start moving. The Sages teach us that a change of space changes our *mazal*, our fate.[2] That may require a move to a new city, refurbishing or repositioning our home furniture, or at least finding ourselves a new place to hang out. Even switching careers or starting a new hobby often works. But does that sound like too much?

The external change does not have to be huge. It's a shift in perspective that's really our aim. Most of the time, going for a walk manages to clear and reorient our thoughts. It's also good to reach out to a person we know will have our best interests in mind. It can be helpful to speak to someone who can reflect back to us our current orientation and introduce to us a refreshing and brand-new point of view. And as any good friend would do, they'll tell us that everyone stumbles into the muddy middle, but with every flop we can become all the more clever; it just takes practice.

The key to becoming more cunning is to first be in touch with our whereabouts. Imagine how that process would begin. We might say, "Oh no, here I am again. I don't know how I got here. I don't remember asking for this. I don't recall stepping into this mess. But now I'm feeling stuck, anxious, and down in the dumps."

It feels awful to be left feeling confused, troubled, and downhearted. Whether or not we've walked down this negative path before, we can at least know our current location. This self-awareness is what allows us to take pause to reflect and redirect. Once we've taken a breath and

---

2. *Shabbos* 6:9.

determined our bearings, we can always recalibrate and firmly put our best foot forward. Stepping out of our negative circumstances takes practice, but the cleverer we get, the easier it becomes.

The Antagonist wants us to feel out of sorts. When we start to feel lost, confused, and disconnected, it's a clear indicator that we've lost track of our whereabouts. When this occurs, it's essential to reestablish our present location. A clever way to do so is by imagining the most recent time we stepped into the muddy middle.

Close your eyes and picture yourself there. Maybe you were alone. If not, think about who was there with you. Do you remember the scene?

This is how we locate our current whereabouts. It's a lot like being frozen in time. We're still there. The memory is alive for us now. It's as if we're still living it in the present moment. If we don't seek this awareness, it'll become our mess; it'll own us, and we'll be bound to relive our struggle over and over again.

So, we become wrapped up in our anxiety, feel melancholic, or lack impulse control. However captivating all that may be, our job in life is way too important to remain gripped by our Antagonist's influence. We must do anything in our power to remove ourselves from the situation.

We must get our legs moving again. Once our legs are activated—and I mean both literally and figuratively—our blood starts to pump and our heart awakens. With this, our Antagonist becomes more transparent, and we begin to grow wiser to its antics. Our eyes see clearly, and we perceive it for what it truly is.

Knowing the true nature of our Antagonist makes us less inclined to repeat its mission. That's the key to begin developing a leopard-like attitude and to start saying with confidence, "I'm sick of you. I know your muddy path is not good for me. I refuse to be led down that dirty road ever again."

King David knows what it means to stumble. His life gives testimony to the clever method in which he removes himself from both external and internal troubles. The more times he manages to cleverly emerge from his predicament, the wiser he becomes.

But does he sound like he's sporting wings? Is he soaring in the air, scoping things out below from a bird's-eye view? No! He's in the midst of it all. He's always caught in the muddy middle. He's in it, every time! Do you know anybody like that? Has anyone ever told you, "I'm stuck. Oh, my goodness. How did I get here? I know I've been here before, and I keep reliving the same old stuff over and over again. I can't get out of this vicious cycle. This is awful. I'm distressed, I'm depressed, I'm anxious. I hate being here. I need therapy."

If so, it's time for him to speak to a spiritual doctor![3] If you know anyone who may be suffering like this, you can remind them that the King of Israel also walked many miles in their shoes. He, too, was caught in the muddy middle. Let your friend know that they don't have a monopoly on this "being stuck, lost, and confused" thing.

Tell them, "You are among royalty!"

TAKEAWAYS

- To become wise, we must first be clever.
- King David's life gives testimony to his clever method of freeing oneself of unhealthy desires, negative external influences, and self-evading pursuits.
- When our thinking is corrupt, our only recourse is to get our legs moving—change our place, change our perspective.
- Feel lost? Imagine the last place you stumbled. You're there again.

---

3. The word "psyche" is defined in Merriam-Webster as a "soul" or "personality." We may deduce from this that psychotherapy is therapy for the soul, and that a psychotherapist's job is to be a spiritual doctor—a healer and practitioner of the soul.

The Schmutz

Chapter 5

Corrective Lenses

O ur eyes are like cameras. When we snap an image of the visual world, it is pictured in the optics of our eye. How the light hits our eyes has much to do with how we perceive the world. Our Antagonist plays with this perception. It plays with our minds and fogs the lenses with which we view the world.

When a lens is caked with too much material, or is made of a dense material, our perception of ourselves and the world around us becomes corrupted.

When do you think these errors in refraction began? Before we were born into this world, our soul was basking in pure joy and spirituality. It was wondrous and whole. There was no excuse to doubt oneself, to be anxious, or to feel down. It was a place of comfort and completeness. We were filled with pure authentic joy. There was nothing to be concerned or worried about.

Subsequently, we were born into the world and we lost sight of what perfection and wholeness look like. It is gone, lost. It disappeared right from underneath our nose, and now we're left with a lifetime of soul searching. Welcome to a life of travail! And one of painstakingly trying to retrieve that which was taken from us.

Does this sound bleak? This happens to be many people's perception of what life has in store for them; in truth, however, this story has been skewed.

I also heard this narrative and spent many years trying to spend every waking hour of the day searching for what it was that I had lost. In addition, I was advised that the solution to this problem was to search deeply and to fastidiously turn over the concepts embedded in Hashem's Torah until I successfully integrated their instructions into my life.

I suppose that's how we're expected to imbue ourselves with the wondrousness that His Torah has to offer. According to this approach, repeatedly going over these lofty lessons is the way Hashem's Torah becomes a part of who we are and the manner in which it influences our field of perception.

If that narrative helps you to become the best version of yourself, great!

If you haven't guessed already, I've always been troubled by the way this narrative was told. It is apparent from the first midrash in *Bereishis Rabbah* that we are cut part and parcel from Hashem's very first thought—His Torah. Our very fabric is designed from its oneness, its wondrousness, and its completeness. We were formed by perfection itself. So, if both our spiritual and organic makeup are fashioned from the very same ethereal material that went into creating Hashem's Torah, how could this deep connection have been forgotten? How could it have been left behind at birth? What kind of birthday present would that really be?

What if I told you that all of the wondrousness that we experienced wasn't really lost, and all the authentic joy and everything we consider most dear to us hasn't truly vanished? You'd probably want to hear the real story.

Here it is: Before we were delivered into the world, we were basking in a realm of splendor, wholeness, and completion. We then received a tap on the lip and subsequently opened our eyes to a brand-new world. But we didn't actually forget our experience. It just got covered up. There's stuff in the way, and it's been hidden from view. As a result of this refraction, our memory and perception of what it means to be whole have become muddied. It became so clouded that we started to believe it's not even there.

It is so concealed that the people we trust the most have even told us that it's gone missing and it's our job to go find it—to retrieve it from wherever it may be hiding.

THE LAYERS OF SCHMUTZ

Have you ever looked around the house for your glasses only to find them already affixed to your face? It's a common phenomenon: a person misplaces something, searches everywhere imaginable, and then is shocked to realize that what they were searching for was sitting right in front of them the whole time.

Your glasses are already affixed to your face. Do you happen to know from where you acquired this particular set of lenses? The lenses we sport directly affect how we define ourselves and engage the world around us. The degree to which we're able to achieve our objectives in life comes down to the style of lenses that we're wearing. It also matters in what direction we're looking. If we've been hyper-focused on externalities, our view of the world has likely become compromised.

It's time to take a look within. When we hesitate, the outside schmutz continues to corrupt our perception, and we're the ones who add to it. Every wrong deed, every deficient act, and every wasted moment leads to an accumulation of the muck. We add layer after layer, concealing who we truly are.

It seems insane that we would add any more to our own bed of schmutz. Aren't our souls covered up enough already?

IT'S TOTALLY CRAZY

If you think this sounds crazy, you're not alone.

The Talmud states, *"Ein adam chotei ela im nichnas bo ruach shtus,"*[1] which literally means that a person doesn't do anything wrong unless a crazy thought enters their mind. A crazy person's mind is distracted. They lack awareness, and it's this feeling of lack that compels them to do the wrong thing. This wrongdoing places another layer of schmutz

---

1. *Sotah* 3a.

over a person's eyes. It's impossible to see the world clearly while look-ing at the world through muddy lenses.

Deficiency is the root of all wrongdoing, and it has been in the world since the beginning of creation. The *Maharal* terms this lacking as *he'edar*, an absence or vacuum.[2] When we feel that there's something missing, it leads to a deep hunger and desire. And if we don't know how to properly guide our hunger, we're more likely to fix our eyes upon the wrong thing and quickly stumble in the wrong direction.

When our vision has been overtaken by a sticky void, our perception becomes significantly altered, and we're bound to consume the very first intriguing thing that crosses before our eyes. Once we fixate on it, it's too late, as Hashem warns: "You will go insane from the vision before your eyes that you see."[3] We're not able to let go of the image that we see, and it takes over our very being. We become convinced that it's something that we severely lack, and we tell ourselves that we can't live without it. Being so crazy about it, how can we not devour it?

Yet, although we feast our eyes upon it, we hardly feel satiated by it. We may have a hunger for it, but because it's not fitting for us, it can barely pass through the gullet. Like young eagles, we suffer from a refraction error of the eye. It is difficult for young eagles to locate fish underneath the water's surface, so they offset this deficiency by fo-cusing on the dead fish that float above. And they still make mistakes, attacking other things such as bobbing seaweed and plastic bottles.

We, too, stare into the middle of murky waters, and we have learned to compensate by grabbing at unhealthy externals. When we abandon our own sense of duty and become satisfied with such surface-level pursuits, that's when we know we've been "hooked and sinkered" by our Antagonist's filthy line.

But as we mature and become cleverer about how to remove the murky film that adulterates our perception, our lenses do start to clear. We start to feel more whole again, and we merit to spot the healthier fish swimming beneath the water's surface.

---

2. *Maharal, Ner Mitzvah*, beginning of chap. 1.
3. *Devarim* 28:34.

CRIPPLING QUAGMIRE

Save me from the mire so I don't sink, that I'll be rescued from my enemies and the deep waters. Don't let the swift current sweep me away, nor the shadowy depths swallow me, and don't let the pit close its mouth over me.[4]

Does it sometimes seem like the earth is swallowing you up? If so, you're most likely feeling down, anxious, or lost. This happens to most of us. It's no great party when you repeatedly find yourself stuck in the quagmire.

The first dirge that we recite on the sad day of Tishah B'Av refers to the habit of toppling into a crippling quicksand, *"bivanis nechuyah,"*[5] that pulls us downward and offers no escape. When we feel down and stuck in life, we are not actually motionless; on the contrary, the job of the quicksand is to pull us down further.

Kind David has chronicled the times that he, too, found himself stuck in this thick mud.[6] He was in a mess of trouble and, as we know, there's simply nothing more uncomfortable than being caught and dragged down by our own set of troubles. Our Antagonist cunningly scoops up this nasty mud and smears it all over our eyes to create a *chatzitzah*, a partition or barrier, between us and the world.[7] The mud creates a smokescreen that clouds the view of our paths, making it all the more possible for our Antagonist to trick us into following its path and not our own.

Sliding down the wrong path is exile personified. It's like we've fallen into a pit and the mouth has closed over us. When the person we truly want to be gets crusted over by this *yavein*, thick and gooey muck, it's easy to lose our bearings. And it is no coincidence that the word *yavein* sounds very much like the word *ye'evein*, which means "to Hellenize." *Yavan* is the Hebrew word for Greece and, as you know, we

---

4. *Tehillim* 69:15–16.
5. Lit., "crippled by quicksand." Rabbi Elazar HaKalir, *Kinnah* #6 in ArtScroll edition.
6. *Tehillim* 40:3 and 69:3.
7. *Mikvaos*, Mishnah 2.

have ample midrashim depicting the Greeks as the masters of darkness and concealment.

You're not the only one who's been Hellenized at one point or another.

It is easy to stumble when the view of the path before us has become obscured and muddled. When King David would find himself in this dark and muddy place, he would look to Hashem to drag him out. After exiting the noxious, murky pit, he would sing a brand-new song, chanting: "He raised one from a [dark] pit of turbulent waters, out of the filthy, muddy mire."[8] The *Metzudas Zion* describes King David's "turbulent waters" as the darkest of pits and characterizes his "filthy, muddy mire" as the gloomiest of all shadowy depths.

When we're not being the best person we can be, it's not unusual to feel off-balance. We're quick to stumble and fall, and once we've tumbled into the quagmire, it's much harder to regain our footing. When King David would find himself in this uncomfortable predicament, he would cry, "I am sunk in the deep mire, and there's no foothold."[9]

It's difficult to maintain independence while being whisked away by negative external forces. It's easy to lose touch with what's important—to slip and get carried away, as King David bemoans, "I have entered the deepest waters, a rushing current sweeps me away."[10] For King David, being stuck in the quagmire isn't just like drowning; it's much worse—swift, tempestuous currents would also oppose him. They would knock him off balance and sweep him away, and any attempt to battle them went awry. His energies would just bounce right back at him. The harder he pushed against them, the harder they pushed back. According to this, when caught in the muddy middle, it's simply not worth putting up a fight.

The term for a rushing current in Hebrew is *shiboles*. It has the same root as *shvil*, an off-the-beaten path that sweeps you away from your very own. When King David felt lost and could no longer find solid ground on his own, Hashem would quickly come to his aid, as he

---

8. *Tehillim* 40:3.
9. Ibid., 69:3.
10. Ibid.

describes: "He set my feet upon a rock; He stabilized my steps."[11] Only with Hashem's help was King David able to regain his balance and stand again upon his own two feet.

The bottom line is that King David had slipped yet again into the muck. He was immobile. He was treading muddy water—his legs were spinning. He was sinking to even greater depths.

Hashem had to step in.

The *Seforno* doesn't think it's prudent to assume that King David was of sound mind when he turned, stumbled, and tumbled into the darkness. Troubleshooting, the *Seforno* suggests that King David "must have been struck with some kind of sickness or disease." Does that mean that King David was also known to lose his mind?

It takes a crazy person to get himself in so far over his head. But when King David was up to his own neck in troubles, an aspect of him always knew to cry out for help, calling, "Save me, Hashem, for the waters have risen up until my soul."[12] The *Seforno* indicates that this precarious situation mirrors the physical challenges of the Babylonian exile (or alternatively, it represents all of the exiles). A physical exile is one thing, but in order to extricate ourselves from a spiritual one, we have to be even more cunning.

Time and time again, Hashem helped him to regain a strong foothold, as King David reminds us: "Who forgives all your wrongdoings; who heals all your diseases?"[13] Only with Hashem's aid was he able to return to a clean bill of health.

We've all felt like King David at one time or another. But being in the clutches of our Antagonist doesn't give it the satisfaction it desires; we just make it hungrier. It drags us down, tosses us around, and tries to get us to feel as far away as possible from ourselves. It does everything in its power to stop us from actualizing our greatest potential.

These moments are inevitable, so the next time we find ourselves in a muddy, muddled moment, we can take King David's lead and give a

---

11. *Tehillim* 40:3.
12. Ibid., 69:2.
13. Ibid., 103:2–3.

holler to Hashem. If not, we won't just feel stuck in the middle of the murky mire. As we said earlier, nobody is really immobile, and there's no such thing as stagnation—we're either moving forward or backward. We're either in or out, moving up or down. This kind of muddy moment is an easy place to get whisked away. And as we've been told, the end of this slippery slope is just a muddy mess of troubles.

WORLD CORRUPTION

A little mud in our eyes can't hurt, right?

> *And the wrongdoers are like the tempestuous sea, for it can't rest, and its waters fling mud and dirt.*[14]

Misdeeds and wrongdoings toss us around. They throw us for a loop and sling mud back into our eyes. Our physical desires strain them, and that's downright uncomfortable.

One thing we learn from King David is to never ask to be tested.

David's eyes were tested. He was confronted with a sight that sealed his destiny. It consumed him, tossing him from the highest spiritual heights to the lowest of the physical lows. You've heard his story: In the darkest of nights, David rose from his bed. He restlessly strolled the palace roof until his eyes were seized by a sight of a story still being told. Like a deer in the headlights, he stood frozen, seeing the most beautiful bathing woman.

She must have been so easy on the eyes to have so easily caught his eye.[15] Like an apple, which tastes soft and mealy at its center, yet appears so pristine on the surface, physical beauty in this world usually only runs skin deep, and it's not always clear what's good for us. Before we recognize its bitter taste, our eyes are already caught feasting upon it. Our eyes are fixed on it and it becomes our pursuit.

It's easy to get dirty in the middle of all the excitement.

---

14. *Yeshayah* 57:20.
15. *Shmuel II* 11:2.

A BAD EYE

It's not our Antagonist alone that places our soul under arrest; we do the same when we judge ourselves and others unfavorably. Just as a bad apple gets rejected from a basket, a *bad eye* propels us into exile. When banished, we're bound to feel all alone and easily lost in a crowd. It's as if we've been plucked and sent out of the world, as Rabbi Yehoshua remarks, "A bad eye, the Antagonist, and the hatred of others remove a person from the world."[16]

Rabbeinu Yonah understands a "bad eye" to be jealousy. Jealousy doesn't just mean being filled with envy when gazing upon someone else's stuff, but worse, it's when we also hold the person in contempt, so that if we don't own it, we don't believe our friend should have it either. Jealousy rears its ugly head by denying our neighbors their possessions or qualities and begrudging their good fortune and accomplishments. Jealous people imprison themselves because they are bound to something foreign—they are striving to walk someone else's path and not their own.

Spending all our precious time trying to have what someone else has and be someone we're not stifles our creativity. We lock our unique gifts and talents away, and if we keep them hidden for too long, they may even wither and decay.

What takes us out of the world? Kicking to the curb the joyous gifts that Hashem has granted us. Rabbeinu Yonah indicates that a person who looks at the world with a bad eye and a crooked lens is not happy with their lot. Trying to "keep up with the Bernsteins" doesn't bode well. Gazing at the material wealth of our friends and wondering when we'll become as wealthy as they are brings suffering our way.

And, speaking of our friends, we simply don't live in a bubble. When we suffer, everyone around us feels it too, and if they're not wise to it, they may even inadvertently experience our pain as if it were their very own.

It's important to note that the Sages indicate that because jealousy is a part of human nature, we have a duty to mute it.

---

16. *Pirkei Avos* 2:11.

In all honesty, desiring that which isn't ours is moot, even if we have the wherewithal to earn it. However hard we try, the burden of jealousy will be too heavy to bear. Our body will weaken, our energy will wane, and we'll find ourselves taken out of this world.

According to the *Rambam*, jealousy blinds us with a heavy darkness. Without light, over time, our eyes atrophy. They become hard and leathered, and everything we gaze upon begins to appear putrid or disgusting.[17] This, he says, leads to a hatred of others.

It's on us. It's our own behavior that transports us out of the world. We make our bed, so it is we who must lie in it. This is not a setup; Hashem isn't punishing us. We become miserable due to our own negative actions. And we're not just left feeling bankrupt, but worse: our Antagonist also conceals all the goodness in life that has been allotted to us. As the Talmud states:

> *Anyone who sets his eyes on something which is not [meant] for him, what he seeks is not given to him, and what is his is taken from him.[18]*

It's a catch-22. Not only do we not get what was never meant for us, but by our own design, we're also denied that which should be coming our way.

> *They sought out many calculations [intrigues].[19]*

King David's son Shlomo is pointing out that the beginning of humanity's frailty stems from a lack of appreciation of our own portion. When we seek to possess that which is outside of our own domain, we're stuck viewing our world from the outside-in.

This is humanity's downfall. When we gaze upon another's honor or possessions, our heart fills with desire, and our conscious mind becomes tormented by inconsistent and conflicting calculations.

---

17. *Rambam, Pirkei Avos* 2:11.
18. *Sotah* 9a.
19. *Koheles* 7:29.

BLIND SPOTS

For a person sees only what appears before his eyes.[20]

Do you have floaters in your eyes? I do. They're microscopic fibers that clump and cast tiny shadows on the retina. I found out that they're permanent, and my mother's friend even claims to have learned to love hers. She's given each one its own special name.

Blind spots are very much like the floaters in our eyes. They mask what's real. We search for what's most valuable but to no avail. Yet again, it's sitting right beneath our nose. How is it that we don't see the obvious when it's right in front of us? Our view is obstructed. We could be staring at the very thing we've been seeking, but our lenses are faulty. All good light is being refracted. Our world is being deflected. It leaves us blind to what's actually good in the world.

And when we manage to allow goodness to slip through, it's doomed to bounce and pass obliquely through the floating, grimy film tacked to our eyelids. The more schmutz that gets in our way, the more numerous our blind spots grow over time. Random fluctuations of data start to muddy our perception. Signals cross, and the good waves are easily misconstrued; the negative looks positive, and what looks negative is actually positive.

---

20. *Shmuel I* 16:7.

Chapter 6

The Eagle Eye

A WISE LENS

Yehudah ben Teima floats like an eagle. He sees the world from a bird's-eye view. As we've said before, he averts his eyes from that which may frustrate him, maintaining a clear view of the path that lies before him. He is truly a wise person.

Imagine what it would be like to see the world through a high-speed, high-definition telescopic lens. Wise people view objects from afar by developing and casting a high-powered telephoto lens, affording them a high magnification and a narrower angle of view. It is wise to develop a keen lens that will allow us to zero in on what truly matters, while keeping the irrelevant and harmful things outside of our line of sight.

In actuality, we're granted this degree of clarity every day. Normally, we have to earn it, but every morning, like clockwork, our lenses are dusted clean. Our eyes are returned to a pristine state. They're no longer obstructed, and we are gifted with a more discerning point of view. Imagine if you could wake up every morning with a fresh start, your vision revitalized, lenses corrected, and everything in your sight crystal clear. You wake up, bat your eyelids, rattle your head, and then realize that your field of perception is no longer encumbered. You're looking at the path before you through a high-definition lens.

It's not our job to rush out every morning to purchase a super-absorbent microfiber cloth to wipe our eyes clean of the nightly schmutz. Instead, it is Hashem who acts as our neighborly optical custodian. When we awaken every morning, it is He who brushes the slumber from our eyes. It's even better than our morning coffee.

And Hashem doesn't just do this for you alone; He extends this gift of clarity to the entire nation of Israel. In truth, He couldn't be a better friend, and that's because He refuses to let us remain amid the nightly dust. He puts an end to the evening schmutz, waking us up bright-eyed, refreshed, and focused—and with a brand-new outlook on life.

Every day, Hashem gives us a fresh opportunity to start anew.

When you wake up in the morning, it is He who is the first to arrive on the scene, showering you with His abundant loving-kindness. This act of loving friendship restores clarity to the whole world—granting you favor, kindness, and mercy from all who gaze upon you.

BETWEEN FRIENDS

Before heading out to synagogue in the morning, we experience and acknowledge this act of loving-kindness by saying our morning blessings. And to shed more light onto this eye-opening phenomenon, it's essential to take a closer look at the relationship that exists between the strongest of friends.

Do you remember the last time you stumbled into the middle of a private conversation? It probably didn't take long to realize that the point that you were trying to interject fell flat; it simply wasn't germane to the discussion at hand. It's difficult to follow the gist of a conversation when we've missed out on its flow from the get-go. The banter that takes place between two friends is even more difficult to discern. It may appear open and playful on the surface, but joining in on the fun will only leave us feeling like an outsider. That's because the space that exists between friends is sacred.

Two friends have the uncanny ability to create an intimate, secure, and understanding environment. The communion between friends is private and contains many veiled themes and nuances. But the relationship as a whole isn't eclipsed; it's strangely noticeable to everyone else around them. Indeed, the amity that exists between friends is in plain view for all eyes to see. An onlooker wouldn't mistake it for anything less than what it appears to be on the surface: a good friendship.

The label we place on a container, shed, or storehouse is based solely on its contents. Friendly discussions are also intimate, confined, and house a lot of private information that is hidden from others. There are many words we could use to describe a private discussion taking place between good friends. What name or title would you give it? What would you call it?

The existing bond between friends plays an important role in the formation of *berachos*, blessings. In order for a blessing to be complete, it must be consistent from start to finish. A blessing that doesn't begin with *"Baruch Atah Hashem"* is considered to be left wide open; it is partial and incomplete. *Baruch Atah Hashem* is a way of saying, "You [Hashem] are the source of all blessing." And when you end a paragraph of blessing with *Baruch Atah Hashem*, it seals the deal, making the blessing complete and whole.

In short, blessings shouldn't be left hanging. That's unfriendly.

The *Tosafos* suggest a clever way to complete a fragmented blessing.[1] The trick is to join it with a blessing that's adjacent to it, that ends in *Baruch Atah Hashem*. The Sages call this solution a *"berachah ha'semuchah l'chaverta,"* literally translated as "a blessing that is next to [or that relies on] its friend." That is how we make a blessing whole and complete, with one central theme from start to finish. The content sandwiched between the two friends is unified, robust, and highly compelling.

If you feel like you're sleeping through life, you should note the following: As we've indicated above, Hashem removes the sleep from our eyes every morning. He wipes the soot clean from our eyelids and provides us with a fresh start and a new perspective, removing the nasty schmutz that's been muddying our perception.

---

1. *Tosafos* on *Berachos* 46a.

In the morning, we thank Hashem for removing the slumber and sleep from our eyes: *Baruch Atah Hashem Elokeinu Melech ha'olam ha'maavir sheinah m'einai u'senumah m'afapai.*

It is worthy of note that most siddurim instruct us not to give an answer to this blessing, that we forgo saying amen. This suggests that in this case, we don't designate a break or create the sort of separation that normally exists between blessings. This way, we're able to narrow the gap, attaching the blessing to the content that immediately follows.

The next paragraph ends with *Baruch Atah Hashem*, but because it doesn't start with this friendly introduction, the Sages were troubled. They therefore decided to apply the *berachah ha'semuchah l'chaverta* principle to resolve the situation. They officially placed the paragraph "next to its friend" by pairing it with the preceding blessing of "removing the sleep from our eyes." This indicates that the content sandwiched between our two juxtaposed *berachos* is held to be particularly sacred.

To get a closer glimpse of what may be Hashem's greater intentions and why He acts so kindly with us every day, let's take a closer look at the content of these two blessings and highlight the central theme they encapsulate.

If you have a moment, grab your siddur and follow along with the translation of the following paragraph. You'll notice that after we recognize that Hashem has kindly eradicated the nightly schmutz from our eyes, we declare:

> *And may it be Your will, Hashem, our G-d, and the G-d of our forefathers, that You awaken us to Your Torah, and attach us to Your mitzvos. Don't bring us into the path of error, nor into the path of missteps and stumbling. Nor into the path of tests, nor into the path of scorn! Don't let our Antagonist dominate us. Distance us from bad-natured people and bad friends [who intend to lead us down the wrong path]. Attach us to our good nature and good deeds and force our good nature to serve You [as we walk our own path]! And grant us today and everyday favor, kindness, and mercy in Your eyes, and in the eyes of all*

who see us. And grant compassionate kindness upon us all.
Baruch Atah Hashem, Who generously grants kindness upon
His people Israel.

Now that we're fully awake, eyes clean and vision cleared, this paragraph provides us with a golden opportunity to ask for guidance. And it's also an opportune time to request that Hashem help us to avoid anything negative that could potentially get in our way. Urging Him to attach us to our good nature and our good deeds, and to place our good nature at the forefront of our mind, empowers us to cling to our path, serving Hashem with all of our might.

And as we see, Hashem's benevolence doesn't just stop with us. He cares for the well-being of all people, and now that He's opened the eyes of the entire world, we're given the opportunity to petition that others find it in their hearts to look favorably upon us as well. Let's face it: we all require a guide to help us channel our own goodness. It's not always so clear what the right thing is to do. By sealing this blessing with the words, "You [Hashem] are the source of all blessing, Who generously grants kindness upon His people Israel," juxtaposed with the theme inherent in the earlier blessing, we can conclude that waking up in the morning and seeing things clearly is itself an act of kindness for us all.

Removing the sleep and soot from our eyes and being able to see things clearly—maybe even for the first time—is a gracious blessing for everyone. We may also infer from the order of the blessing that in order to successfully channel our bad nature for the good, we're first required to view ourselves and the world around us through spot-free lenses.

The problem is that schmutz settles on our eyes during the night, and it muddies our perception. The Talmud refers to sleep as one-sixtieth of death and, suffice it to say, if it weren't for Hashem's help, we'd wake up dead to the world.[2]

But how do we usually show our gratitude?

We all hunger for a daily ounce of clarity, and Hashem grants it to us every morning. In truth, the rest of the day is on us. We actually have to

---

2.   *Berachos* 57b.

earn it. And that's because after waking up wide-eyed, lenses unclouded and unrestricted, we quickly lose sight and often stumble right into the muddy middle. Before we know it, we're spending the duration of the day tossing soot and dust right back into our eyes.

It's a dirty trick.

TAKEAWAYS

- When our lenses are caked with schmutz, it messes with the perception we have of ourselves and the world around us.
- Nobody does anything wrong unless a crazy thought enters his mind.
- In murky waters, we compensate by reaching for unhealthy externals. Trying to possess that which is outside of our own domain means we're unhappy with our lot.
- We're always on the go, moving either forward or backward.
- The more schmutz that gets in our way, the more numerous our blind spots grow over time, and the more distorted our view. What's negative looks positive, and what looks negative is actually positive.
- When Hashem wakes us up in the morning and wipes the soot from our eyes, our field of perception is no longer encumbered with the schmutz, and we are thus granted a fresh start and a new perspective.

SECTION IV

Your
Whereabouts

Chapter 7

Power of Distinction

A re you feeling out of whack? If so, you're probably off-balance, a bit distressed, and have fallen out of bounds. You've lost sight of your own limits; your boundaries are off-kilter.

This is because you've somehow lost track of your *whereabouts*.

Regaining an awareness of our whereabouts is essential for our psychological health. This idea is discussed in Dr. Fritz Perls' book, *The Gestalt Approach and Eye Witness to Therapy*. He indicates that a person who feels out of whack and has lost their capacity to differentiate between one thing and another has a duty to reestablish this faculty.

In his opinion, it is the therapist's job to help you to rediscover yourself while at the same time provide clarity into what surely isn't yourself, what fulfills you, and what thwarts you. According to Dr. Perls, we need to be guided toward integration. This requires seeking assistance in order to find the proper balance and determining the boundary point that exists between ourselves and the world around us.[1]

There's a world out there, and it's important to be able to distinguish between it and ourselves. In order to achieve that, we must first locate our own *whereabouts*. In the following anecdote, you'll witness the difficulty Jack had in trying to find himself amid all his anxiety and doubt.

---

1.   Fritz Perls, *The Gestalt Approach and Eye Witness to Therapy* (Bantam Books, 1981), p. 43.

BEING MYSELF

Jack had just returned to dating after a six-month hiatus. He was very anxious and expressed a lot of hesitation about going on his first date. He was plagued with doubt.

The following discussion illustrates how he was able to overcome doubt by unleashing his *power of distinction*.

At the beginning of our talk, Jack was overflowing with uncertainty and fear. He stated, "I'm afraid I'm not going to be myself." He was bubbling with worries and what-ifs, wondering, "What if it doesn't work out? How do you even know when you're supposed to get engaged? Maybe I'm not good enough. Maybe I won't like her at all."

We spoke at length about the power of doubt and his inability to differentiate.

His biggest fear was that he wouldn't be himself on the date. This gave me good reason to be alarmed. I asked myself, *If he isn't going to be himself on the date, then who will he be?*

I proceeded to sketch out onto a piece of paper the following "Being Myself" spectrum and asked him to draw an "x" where he currently saw himself on the spectrum. Truth be told, I was curious, and I wanted some convincing. He seemed to be aware of times that he wasn't himself, so I wanted to check if he could pinpoint himself actually being himself right there in the moment.

As you may have imagined, Jack marked an "x" closer to the *Not Feeling Like Myself* end of the spectrum. It's important to note that people are unable to harness their power of distinction while caught feeling sidelined because that's when they're not feeling altogether like themselves. The tension, stress, and discomfort that accompany this are a call to action!

It is my job to first make sure that a person is fully present with me in the room. So, with slight tongue in cheek, I mentioned to Jack how preposterous it all sounded to me—the fact that there are actually times in life when people believe that they're not being themselves. If so, who in the world was sitting before me in the room? How could anyone not be themselves?

Looking back at his Being Myself spectrum, Jack admitted with a shake of the head, "It sounds totally ludicrous." Yet people still feel this way.

It's helpful to remember that no matter how distant we may feel from being the person we truly want to be, we can always locate ourselves somewhere along our very own Being Myself spectrum.

It doesn't take long to realize that when we're not being ourselves, it's still us; we're simply being the particular aspect of ourselves that doesn't like being ourselves.

LIFE PRESERVER

Jack spoke at length about his anxiety. He was riddled with it. He claimed that it was the one thing he felt was holding him back from being fully himself.

Are you familiar with the famous parable of the *life preserver*? When a person is feeling lost or out of sorts, the chest tends to tighten and breathing becomes labored. An episode like this is often likened to the experience of drowning, and that's when it makes sense to reach for a life preserver. We feel that our life is in danger and even if it only helps for a brief moment, clutching onto it makes us feel safe and secure. Jack's cycle of anxiety was propelling him into a mode of preservation. The more anxious he felt, the less he perceived himself to be himself. And the more it bothered him, the more anxious he became.

It's nearly impossible to locate our whereabouts when stuck in preservation mode. For Jack, anxiety had become both a place of refuge and the very thing he wanted to flee. The moment he sensed a pang of anxiousness, he would instinctively try to protect and fortify himself. And what was it that he'd grab onto? That's right—he would latch onto his old and reliable feelings of anxiety.

POWER OF PRESERVATION

The moment that we deny any part of ourselves, we form a gap between the different aspects of who we are. Life becomes blurry, and we deprive ourselves of the ability to differentiate. We might not like it, but the lack of recognition of this part of ourselves sends us to a particularly memorable location. It catapults us right into the muddy middle.

And that's when we can be sure that our power of preservation has fully kicked in.

What sort of steps can we take to get out of preservation mode? A clever way out is to first embrace the aspect of yourself that wants to avoid being yourself. Once you've reintegrated yourself with the rest of yourself, your anxiety will magically dissipate.

Don't get me wrong: there's a real benefit to feeling incomplete and torn apart. The emotional and physical stress that we experience while in a state of preservation is not for naught. It has the power to sharpen our perception. It alerts us to the fact that although we thought we were perilously drowning, we can rest assured that we're still very much alive and kicking.

Our distress, disorder, and difficulty also provide us with natural benefits. Let's say we mistakenly step out onto the road into oncoming traffic. The moment we feel distressed and become anxious, our power of preservation quickly swoops to the rescue and gets our adrenaline pumping.

The power of preservation is the force that tells the body to jump out of the way of the oncoming car. Thank goodness for our instincts. (And to boot, leaping off the road and surviving such a precarious event is sure to always make a great story!)

Further, it really leaves an impression—it doesn't take long for our subconscious mind to learn that this particular coping mechanism can also be applied to future events. We just have to learn how to guide it. Without awareness, we have no way of knowing whether it's being used for the good or for the bad.

Let's say you know you have an important meeting tomorrow. If you're like Jack, feelings of what-if and your fear of the unknown will likely begin to flutter. That's the very moment when your Antagonist will show up and declare, "Hey, Jack, you don't want to be yourself right now."

That's how we know when our power of preservation has stopped working in our favor. The quicker we catch on to this possible overstep, the wiser we become.

BEEN THERE, DONE THAT

Now that Jack was fully present in the room, we were able to move on and discuss his long-term goal of learning how to manage his feelings of doubt. The unique thing about doubt is that it is our Antagonist's doing. It's not who we are, but a foreign idea filled with ill intentions.

Jack decided that being in control of his thoughts would be a good first step. As long as he could push the doubt aside, he could ignore its influence. The following is a wonderful case of "been there, done that."

Jack came back the next week and indicated that he'd given doubt some thought. He said, "I did all the work in my head." He succeeded at giving it distinction and started to see it as its own thing—an entity in and of itself. He recognized it as having its own power and hoped this would be the first step toward letting it go.

"The date went well," he reported.

Just as soon as he began sharing his dating experience, his penchant for uncertainty resurfaced. He began to obsess, wondering, "What does she want? What is she actually looking for?" Worrying about all this future stuff made him noticeably anxious. I sat in silence with him. Suddenly, with bright blue eyes he miraculously declared, "This is my obsession with anxiety coming back!"

Jack started to see his anxiety for what it truly was. He realized that his Antagonist was just using it as a tool to knock him off-balance and throw him off track. In order to clearly see our adversary's shenanigans, like Jack, we need to utilize our tool of *daas*, our power of distinction.

The *Rambam*, in the *Mishneh Torah*, teaches that we are imbued with this power of distinction at birth.[2] It is our power of distinction that

---

2. *Mishneh Torah, Yesodei HaTorah*, chap. 1.

gives us the ability to see our Antagonist for what it truly is and also allows us to see ourselves as a whole being—an independent entity.

Setting ourselves apart is what transforms us into a real mensch. Distinguishing ourselves from the noisy crowd gives us the veneer of being both efficient and self-sufficient. You have what it takes to be your own person. There's nothing greater than being self-assured of your own whereabouts.

TAKEAWAYS

- It is important to differentiate between who we are and the world around us.
- There is a particular aspect of yourself that doesn't like being yourself, but it's still a vital part of yourself.
- Our struggle has the potential to become both our foe and our life preserver.
- Denying any part of ourselves forms a gap between the different aspects of ourselves, depriving us of the ability to differentiate and catapulting us into a state of personal discord.
- When we feel distressed and anxious, our power of preservation quickly swoops to our rescue.
- Our power of distinction permits us to see our Antagonist for what it really is—and to see ourselves as a whole being, and an independent entity.

Chapter 8

Persona Non Grata

OUTSIDE-IN

The awareness of how embracing unhealthy externalities affects a person negatively has also permeated the modern world of psychology. Dr. Fritz Perls, the developer of Gestalt therapy, warns that if we take an outside-in approach, we're bound to "incorporate into ourselves standards, attitudes, and ways of acting and thinking, which are not truly ours."[1]

What's the problem with soliciting this external persona non grata? Inviting the outside world into our inner world is a form of what Dr. Perls calls *introjection*. This apparent lack of boundaries imperils our very core, as he warns: "In introjection, we have moved the boundary of the world so far inside ourselves that there is almost nothing left of us."[2] When we don't have a mind of our own, it's like we're a nobody. And when we're a nobody, we lack a world of our very own.

It's possible to completely lose our whereabouts when approaching the world from the outside-in.

---

1. *The Gestalt Approach and Eye Witness to Therapy*, pp. 34–35.
2. Ibid.

INSIDE-OUT

To be one step ahead of our Antagonist, we need to follow King David's lead and start to approach life from the inside-out. The decision-making process, and the choices that we make in life, must start from within the inner chambers of our heart.

How do we create a healthy set of lenses with which we can view our outer world? As we've already determined, our eyes are very impressionable. This is something every wise person knows. Working from the inside-out inspires our heart to guide our eyes in a more favorable direction. When done right, it awakens our healthy desires and helps us to realize what we truly value in life.

Over time, it becomes easier to limit our scope, and we begin to zero in on the good parts. We only allow the right messages to filter in, focus on the best in people, and begin to illustrate in our minds the necessary positive images that help us to reach our life goals.

According to Rabbi Chaim Friedlander—the famed educational director at Yeshivas Ponovezh—in his book *Mesilas Chaim B'Chinuch*, the manner in which we perceive our world is a pedagogical one. We've been bombarded with an outside-in approach from the outset. Since the very first moment that we opened and batted our eyelids, our parents, extended family, and other outside influencers have tried to shape our reality. I am sure they always meant well, but human beings do make mistakes. When our influencers try to shape our reality in ways that don't speak directly to our heart, a dense layer of external schmutz builds up, and it can take years to maneuver our way out.

Western culture promulgates an outside-in approach as well. We're living in very superficial times, where people are constantly worried about how things appear on the surface. The lifestyles of the rich and famous are more about aesthetics than authentic personal values, meaning, and growth. Movies, television, and the fashion industry dictate how we and our children should look and behave. We perceive and rate ourselves based on the images we see and the messages they provide. Negative outside forces are quick to usurp our personal ambition and misdirect our unique energies. Be aware: any battle that we unleash against these forces is only in *reaction* to their powerful nature and influence.

It's easy to slip into preservation mode when we sense that our basic values are being disrespected or disregarded. This reactive approach is bound to spill over, muddying our personal relationships and corrupting the perception we have of the world around us.

When we're not taking a proactive stance to the outside world, we're stuck living an outside-in cycle of life.

Our current educational system is no exception. Rabbi Chaim Friedlander concurs that the most common educational style can be described as an outside-in approach.[3] All teachers hope to have a positive influence on their students, but the real point of contention is how one chooses to relate the information to them in the first place. It doesn't matter how sharp-witted a person may be; it's always difficult for an educator to get an idea across and to successfully communicate it in a way that it will directly enter another person's heart. How do you take wisdom and inject it into someone else's heart?

The common outside-in approach demands that students study and learn to incorporate information on their own. In this case, students tend to do better when provided with the study tools and the guidance necessary to learn and retain the information. However we look at it, this approach requires the student to do most of the work.

Obviously, the instructor wants us to mull the information over, which requires repeatedly reviewing it until we can claim it as our own. Once we come to fully understand the information, we're expected to inculcate it into our very being. It then has the ability to enlighten us, influence our perception of reality, and ultimately affect who we are as people.

Unfortunately, this style of learning can often leave a person feeling handicapped. It can be misleading, primarily because we are likely to stop looking inward for answers. It can fool us into thinking that

---

3. *Mesilas Chaim B'Chinuch*, p. 97.

connecting to outside sources and ideas is the only way to learn, grow, and develop ourselves.

If you can relate to this phenomenon, it's most likely because you sense that your internal creative powers and intuitive technical know-how were hijacked somewhere along the way. If so, it is possible that what you honestly value has been masked by living and learning strictly from the outside-in.

INSIDE-IN

I would have thought that the opposite of an outside-in modus operandi would be an inside-out approach, but according to Rabbi Friedlander, the ability to truly connect and relate to another person demands an inside-in perspective. This approach places the ball in the hands of the instructor. The assumption is that a teacher can't move anyone further than he has moved himself; the teacher has to do the work first.

It's only after we've sufficiently turned over the material to the point at which it has become a part of ourselves that we're now fit to teach it over to another. Our efforts to master the material ignite our hearts and allow us to pay it forward. This is by far the most direct route for the dissemination of information. It is a delivery system that works from the inside to the inside. In short, it's a heart-to-heart.

It is time to cultivate your inner power and to awaken yourself to yourself. I'm not suggesting an outward display, a big performance, or some type of public exhibition. Personal transformation is meant to be a private endeavor.

After awakening yourself to the wisdom that's living within your heart, you may then reach out to the people closest to you and seek to unlock a doorway into their hearts as well.

TAKEAWAYS

- Adopting an outside-in approach moves the boundary of the world so deep inside of ourselves that almost nothing of us remains.

- It is essential to learn what healthy messages to allow in, to focus on the best in people, and to illustrate in our mind positive images in order to reach our life goals.
- An inside-in approach assumes that we can't move anyone further than we've moved ourselves.
- Personal transformation is a private matter.
- The best way to transfer information is by having a heart-to-heart.

Chapter 9

Patterns

*I don't know who to turn to or where to go. I don't know
where I'm headed anymore. I've lost track of what's
important. I'm tired of feeling stuck. I don't know how
I got into this mess. How do I get out of here, and even
if I do, how can I be sure that I won't just fall right back
into this negative state all over again?*

If any of those phrases sound familiar to you, it's totally normal,
and it stinks when you're having such a hard time. You're right in
the middle of it. And I know, it always seems eternal when you're
stuck smack-dab in the muddy middle.

People go through difficult periods in their lives. Are you starting to
see a pattern? Maybe you're tired of seeing the same old themes resurface in your life. It's frustrating when you can't seem to move on.

There are some people who appear to "keep on keeping on." They
stride forward. Whether they're stuck in a negative state for a few
hours, a couple of days, weeks, or months, they do seem to eventually
break out of their unhealthy pattern. There's an end, and once they
reach it, they move on. But for them, moving on means falling back
into their old routine.

Does that really sound like a clean exit? In spite of the fear of getting stuck all over again, these people do seem able to continue on with their lives, and I wonder what tools and guiding principles they're implementing to be able to so easily stride onward. But that said, aren't they still afraid of returning to and falling prey to their greatest concerns? If so, this may be an indicator that they've never really broken the chain. Maybe it's all just a pattern. They decide to move forward, subsequently fall into the middle of the muck, get stuck, and when they somehow—miraculously—get themselves unstuck, they continue forward until they lose balance and stumble all over again.

FORESEEABLE PATTERNS

A good diagnostician knows that the trick to identifying a person's greatest concerns comes down to foreseeable patterns. How many times do we need to do something before it can be considered a pattern in our life?

Maybe one action is enough to put things into motion. One infusion may be all it takes to give us the fuel necessary to repeat it. This would be well and good if it were a positive action, but Ben Azai adds in the Mishnah that the flip side is also disturbingly true: the consequence of doing a negative act is doing another one.[1]

As a result of our initial negative action, Rabbeinu Yonah explains that a severe gap forms between ourselves and Hashem. All it takes is but a split second to quickly forsake what is most important in our lives. We may conclude from this that one negative act is all it takes to toss an iron wrench into our efforts to realize our life's potential. It's no wonder that this causes us to feel torn, distant, and thoroughly *farmisht*.[2]

It's this existential residue that makes it more likely that we will repeat such a self-defeating act.

"At this point, what do you really care? You're already feeling out of sorts. Just go ahead and do it (again)!" your Antagonist persists.

---

1. *Pirkei Avos* 4:2.
2. *Farmisht*: Yiddish word meaning "mixed up," "confused," or "crazy."

But Hashem wants us to choose life! In line with Rabbeinu Yonah, Hashem doesn't place good or bad into our hands, but choice alone. Hashem stresses this by commanding:

> *I have set before you life and death, the blessing and the curse.*
> *You shall choose life, so that you and your offspring will live.*[3]

He wants us to choose what's best for us. If we choose well, we've chosen life. When we choose to walk a good path, Hashem walks it with us. When we do the right thing, He helps make it easier for us to do another.

But when we slip up, a vacuum forms between us and Hashem, and this opens us up to the ill-fated powers inherent in the outside world. The experience of being stuck in a negative flow can be explained by simple physics: when we stumble, we're slated to stumble again, and that's because of the inertia we've created with the initial negative act.

Rav Ovadia mi'Bartenura explains that this is our reward. Our reward for doing the first negative act is a golden opportunity to do another. Additionally, he states that we get credit for both the benefit and pleasure that we receive from doing the initial wrong deed. Making a poor decision, and also enjoying its benefits, is what ultimately rewards us with another. In other words, we slipped up and enjoyed it, and now we're in double trouble.

We earned our reward! It's the fruit of our labor. We're a success, slated to continue our ill-driven actions. But in truth, it's lonely at the top.

Rabbeinu Yonah reveals that if we choose the bad, Hashem will distance Himself from us. As long as we're completely married to our bad actions, Hashem wants no part in them. But we really don't have to be alone. Once we're caught in this negative flow, and we find it nearly impossible to get out on our own, we can always utilize our *power of return*. The power is in our hands to turn ourselves right around—and run directly home.

---

3.   *Devarim* 30:19.

POWER OF RETURN

None of us enjoy feeling the pangs of regret over our private mistakes, but they're often the best motivators to start harnessing our *power of return*. We may bounce back on track just by following three thoughtful steps.

- The first step is to decide in our heart that a particular behavior isn't befitting a person like ourselves. We know it's second-rate and repeating it wouldn't be prudent. We may even find ourselves saying, "I'm not the sort of person who would do such a thing." We can be self-assured that this one misstep does not have to lock us into a pattern. It doesn't have to represent the person we've been striving to be all along.
- The second step is to mourn the person we think we've become. This allows us the time to take pause to recalibrate and imagine ourselves becoming the person we truly want to be.
- The third step turns us right around. It returns us to our initial state. But this step is tricky; reaching ground zero requires much fortitude. When we are confronted with the very same challenge again, we must decide to not repeat the initial act. A wise person will say, "I'm not going there again. I'm staying far away from that unhealthy thought or behavior. I'm sticking to what's best for me."

It's not just the same old story with a positive twist in the end. It's our return ticket home. It's a brand-new story. And as its author, we may confidently use this fresh start to place our right foot forward and to begin living more authentically. There should be no need to look back after making the decision. We can simply view that old negative action as a common hiccup, a small blip in the greater scheme of life. It was a one-off and nothing has really been altered.

Achieving this means that we have a *chezkas kashrus*—we're still kosher. We have successfully reached ground zero. Once there isn't any proof of our past deeds—we haven't caused ourselves any irreversible damage—we're considered to be what's called *muchzack*, meaning, we haven't changed our standing in the least. We automatically fall back into our original, default status. We slide ourselves right back into home plate. A wise person knows that one overstep doesn't have to mean that a reoccurrence is inevitable.

In truth, we can crack any bad habit by mobilizing our power of return. It's simply easier to bounce back when negativity hasn't been given the time to take hold. The more habituated we've become, the cleverer we need to be to shake our unhealthy ways.

HABITUATION

When does an action start to take hold and really become a habit? With enough heedlessness and measured dedication, our negative actions can take full hold. Nonetheless, between implementing a bit of self-awareness and our power of return, one misstep does not need to be habit-forming. Adopting any new practice demands a certain amount of time and effort. It doesn't have to be a huge endeavor, but to integrate a new way of being into our daily lives, we have to give it at least a couple of tries.

A Talmudic discussion between Rabban Shimon ben Gamliel and Rebbi reveals that repeating something two to three times is all it takes to establish a fixed pattern:[4]

- According to Rebbi, an action becomes habitual when it has been repeated twice under the very same conditions.
- Rabban Shimon ben Gamliel requires three times in order to really make it stick.

That's how easily a negative action can become a part of our reality. Replicating it just a few times is enough to cause the changeover. The real turning point, though, is when we begin to define ourselves by it. This means that, for whatever reason, we've started to own it and fully dedicate ourselves to it. We see a reflection of this idea in the language we use. Some people feel like they should share the news of their bad deeds with the world. Western society respects those who admit, or "own up to," their deeds.

---

4.   *Niddah* 64a.

According to the Talmud, if we've managed to hold onto a parcel of land that we inherited or acquired for three full years, we're believed to be the owner of that land. We're able to say, "I'm a landowner, and hey, that's my land." It can't be disputed.

But let's say we have no deed, no contract, or any proof of purchase. If the original owner comes and claims, "Hey, I was just renting it to you," and we haven't reached our three-year mark, we can't claim it as our own. We may even owe them a pretty penny for a portion of the produce that we've grown and sold.

The three years grant us security and enable us to treat the land as if it was ours all along. We can define ourselves by it and continue to invest our time in it, and nobody else can dispute it.[5] Similarly, once we're convinced that we fully own our behavior, start to define ourselves by it, and dedicate most of our time to doing it, there's no apparent reason to dispute it. And why would we? It grants us a welcome degree of certainty and security.

THEMES

How do patterns play out as themes in our narrative?

Let's say that you've repeated a negative action at least three times. How would you describe yourself now? It's important to be really specific because this will be the governing theme in your story. Would you say you've been feeling down, anxious, stressed, or out of control as of late? Maybe you're haunted by doubts, struggling with making decisions, or just downright frustrated. If so, is this a new thing for you, or has it been a concern in your life for a while?

If you're apt to find yourself in this same situation over and over again, then you know it's become a running theme in your life's script.

Has anyone ever chided you, "Nu, why don't you just get over it?" If you already recognize that this behavior has become a pattern, you're ahead of the curve. We do get tired of seeing the same old negative themes resurface in our lives, and it is frustrating when we can't seem

---

5. *Bava Basra* 35a.

to move on. We're rough on ourselves when we see other people moving forward in life with ease.

But is that their real story? It may be true for a select few, but like we said before, most people are stuck in one negative state or another. Even if they appear to miraculously break out of their vicious cycles, it doesn't necessarily mean they've done the work that will keep them going in the right direction. Returning to what they consider to be their normal routine is categorically still a part of their negative ebb and flow. It may be a place of contentment for them, but like any other negative pattern, they're destined to find themselves standing before the same precipice in the near future.

This is how some people's themes always play out. They may be adept at walking away from negativity, but they often struggle to create the necessary disconnect. Anxiety, depression, and the need to feed one's addiction could be crouching just around the corner, and somehow certain people are able to continue living normal and fulfilling lives. It is truly remarkable that one can remain firm in spite of such impending doom. The chaotic nature of their lives is composed of a recycled theme. This is what some experts refer to as "organized chaos," meaning, they may experience life as chaotic, but they're really just stuck hovering in a fixed pattern.

When life has become predictably unpredictable, it has its benefits. That's because it has become our norm. When treading in muddy waters, we can fall back on our old routine.

YOUR NORM

There's security in having a routine. It works. It's reliable. It's your modus operandi, and nobody else can take that away from you. It's your norm.

Why would we even want to make a change? Maybe this is the quality of life for which we've always hoped. But if we're feeling negative about it, what keeps us doing it? After a few cracks at doing a negative behavior, we do succeed in actualizing some of its potential. No matter how unhealthy it may be, it does appear to have become a part of our very being. The manner in which we think about it, and the degree to which we're committed to maintaining it, have become a fetter for life's most important and pressing decisions. As strange as it may sound, this unhealthy behavior makes us feel productive; it gives our life purpose! Not only has it become accepted, it's expected. To a great extent, we've become enslaved by it. It has a foothold in every life decision we make. It's become our point of reference, the lens through which we view our world and the world around us.

When our negative patterns become our norm, they become very difficult to oppose. While initially, these behaviors make us feel uncomfortable, ashamed, or guilty, over time, they no longer appear negative and begin to take on a whole new meaning. When we're not wise to this change, we start to redefine ourselves by them in a new way. We rewrite our narrative to fit their newly scripted purpose, remaining blind to their nefarious plan.

THE THIRD LINK

So, you're stuck in a negative groove. Many people are. Does that mean your next move is going to be just another link in the chain?

We've established that doing an action three times transforms it into a reality—into our reality. And the more often we come to repeat it, the more it clouds our worldview. The *Maharal* likens our third act to the third link in a chain.[6] Every additional link has the potential to darken our perception. We may easily be duped into thinking that every new link is just another loop in a series of bad actions. But is our behavior really that predictable? Are all events necessarily linked to one another?

Unhealthy behavior is but a direct result of our first actions, and due to this, our Antagonist makes every effort to convince us that this third link means we're doomed to repeat the action, but in truth, the Antagonist is only yanking our chain.

To the wise eye, this third link is looser than it appears. Although it's an outgrowth of the initial two, it has the capacity to be both connected and disconnected from them through and through. Although the second link in the chain is undoubtedly linked to the first, and the third

---

6. *Tiferes Yisrael*, vol. 3, end of chap. 50.

directly to the second, the third link is so distant from the first that it's become something entirely new—brand-new.

When we're tired of reliving the same old negative patterns in life, the third link in the chain is our ticket out. Since we can view our behavior as disconnected from our initial act, we can use this built-in, fail-safe method to stop the flow. Without this tool, we'd inevitably be stuck feeling like just another link in the chain. Thanks to the distance between the first and third link, any desire to continue our behavior is now going to be solely based on a totally new and different reason; it can't help but serve a new function. Although the first two links are what helped us arrive at this new state, the new break in flow gives us the opportunity to recalibrate and decide whether to continue this mode of behavior from here on in.

The inherent disconnect is what permits us to do the wise thing. The distance gives us pause, providing us the space necessary to place our focus inward. We may then ask ourselves, "Why am I still doing this? Is continuing this action really in my best interests? Is it who I am? Is this what I truly value?" It's normal to think that we're always going to be stuck in the flow and that we are destined to forever be linked to our first actions. But we don't have to be ruled by inertia. At any point, we may take pause to reflect, reorient, and redirect. The wise person knows that no matter how many links down the chain he may be, he can always stop to inquire, "Is it worth continuing with this particular behavior or thought pattern?"

You don't have to be chained to your past thoughts and actions. We own the ability to set ourselves free. Thanks to this fail-safe, we may unleash our *power of imagery*, and imagine ourselves boldly snipping away at the chain with a pair of ethereal metal cutters.

We're far removed from whatever linked us to our past in the first place. In line with the *Maharal*, it's even become a brand-new animal. We get to decide whether to feed it or not. In order to stride forward, the wise person views this negative behavior as ancient history. It's just an old story, and that's what makes it all the more possible to leave it behind.

TAKEAWAYS

- There are people who appear to keep on keeping on, but for them, moving on really means that they're just falling back into their old routine.
- Choosing what's in our best interest is choosing life!
- A wise person knows that one misstep doesn't have to mean that he is bound to relive it.
- It takes two to three tries under the same conditions for an action to take full hold.
- There's safety to routine, so why change?
- We don't have to be stuck feeling like just another link in the chain.

The Daily Grind

Chapter 10

The Hungry Bear

He created the wild beast on earth; He created the wild beast in humanity.[1]

THE BEAST WITHIN

The words of the serpent piqued the curiosity of the first woman, asserting, "You will not die, for Hashem knows that on the day that you eat of it, your eyes will be opened and [just like Hashem ate from the tree] you will be like Him, knowing good and bad."[2] When her gaze fell upon the lovely fruit, she was instantly smitten, as Hashem's Torah reveals: "And the woman saw that the tree was good for eating and that it was a delight to the eyes."[3] She gave the fruit to her husband, and when he ate from it, both of their eyes were held wide open.[4] Bad was seen all around them and they hungered for

---

1. *Avos D'Rabi Nosson*, chap. 31.
2. *Bereishis* 3:5; see *Rashi*.
3. *Bereishis* 3:6.
4. Ibid., 3:7.

it. It was as if a beast with a strong desire to consume everything in the world, both bad and good, was planted inside of them.[5]

This hungry monster is strangely reminiscent of the second beast that the prophet Daniel envisioned in his dream. He envisaged, "Then behold! Another beast, a second one, similar to a bear; it was placed on one side, and there were three ribs in its mouth between its teeth; and this is what they said to it, 'Arise, devour much flesh!'"[6]

Giving us a glimpse into the prophet's vision, Rav Yosef describes a creature that desires food and drink, and is as woolly as a bear. It is never satisfied and is constantly on the prowl, without rest. It is a hungry, wandering bear.[7] In other words, it's a consumer—the greatest ever. And it won't stop until it has swallowed up everything in the universe.

INNER HUNGER

When we feel that something is missing and we sense an empty pit in our heart, we are bound to experience an inner hunger. This hunger triggers a hankering which is difficult to curb. When we're craving something, our hungry bear takes hold, and our only concern is to fill the empty hole. This causes many people to go out on the prowl.

According to Rabbi Eliyahu Dessler, hunger is basically a reaction to a weakness or discomfort that's triggered by an existing inner deficiency. "Hunger isn't life itself," he clarifies, but is just there to give us the necessary boost to stay alive.[8] He adds that whether "for good or for bad," our different appetites are "emissaries of our heart's inclinations." Namely, our desires are an outgrowth of an emptiness that pangs somewhere within the chambers of our heart.

The downside to our appetites is that they often send us down the wrong path. And it doesn't help that they are so incredibly relentless. It's hard to stop them dead in their tracks. Once we feel hungry, we don't just hunger for now. Intensified by what *might* happen, our hunger perks

---

5. Ibid., 2:25, *Rashi; Bereishis Rabbah* 19:9.
6. *Daniel* 7:5.
7. *Kiddushin* 72b.
8. *Strive for Truth*, vol. I, p. 133.

its enthusiasm, gearing us up for any potential consumption down the road. And there's no end to this desire. The hungry beast will never be satisfied. And the more that we attempt to indulge its cravings, the more intense our hunger becomes. This is what makes the hungry bear the most miserable of creatures.

Your Lot

Why are we so doggedly determined to fulfill our desires? Maybe it's because we're not satisfied with our lot.

Isn't it all for naught? No matter how ambitious we are about feeding our appetites, we're never going to fully make our mark. There's no such thing as being totally fulfilled in this world, as the midrash teaches: "No person leaves this world with half of their desires fulfilled."[9] So why do we keep on latching onto things that don't serve our best interests? Attaching ourselves to something that isn't fitting for us just leads to more psychological pain and unnecessary tension.

In line with Rabbi Dessler, what we're doing is beastly. We're acting like an animal that's attempting to mark its territory. We're trying to extend our personal domain—we want to get our hands on that which is outside of ourselves simply *because it's outside of ourselves.*[10]

Maybe it's time we got into our thick woolly heads that what we're already receiving is enough. What we're hungry for lies nearby, and our efforts to explore outside ourselves are in vain. We'd be better off expending all this hungry energy trying to find answers from within. The heart's intentions can either be for the good or for the bad, which means there's an upside to having an inner hunger: we can direct all of our spirited ambition toward doing good things in the world!

The hungry bear yearns to feel satisfied, and it will be on the prowl until it has consumed pretty much everything. In other words, it wants to gain control of the entire physical environment. If given the wherewithal, it would expand its influence to all four corners of the earth.

---

9. *Koheles Rabbah* 1:34.
10. *Strive for Truth*, vol. I, p. 137.

Our inner hunger is no different. The heart yearns to reach beyond itself, and this can be used for the positive. Our legs are just itching to run to do goodness in the world. We have a natural inclination to want to do the right thing for ourselves and for the people around us. That's a much more noble reason to take our hunger global!

Need for Attachment

Have you considered that maybe your hunger has a spiritual side? The bear cub in us wants to fulfill its need for attachment. The pangs of emptiness that we experience are actually there to inspire us to want to connect to something much greater than ourselves. Our soul is reaching out, and we are yearning to cling to the infinite.

As long as we are not satisfied with our portion, we are slated to stay on the prowl, so it's in our better interests to start directing our ambition toward healthier and more spiritual pursuits. The more ambitious we are about performing acts of kindness for others, the more successful we are at satisfying our own need for attachment.

When we make a wholehearted effort to do good in the world, it doesn't just stop there. Doing good things for others gets us juiced up and energizes us to want to do more. And our friends benefit from this as well, because they also have a need for attachment.

It's important to be mindful when seeking attachment. If we're not fully on the ball, our Antagonist will make every effort to trick us into latching onto the wrong things. It will distract us into tasting its sweet nothings. How does it lure you into its sticky trappings? By placing them just a bit outside of your immediate realm.

The Antagonist, knowing that we're naturally drawn toward externals, sugarcoats everything. It hopes we won't hesitate to wrap our sticky claws around that which is found directly outside of ourselves.

The Honeytrap

The honeypot—it's a trap. Be warned of its perils. Acting on our desires can easily veer us off track, and if we're not careful, we'll go right to pot. We're bound to totally lose ourselves in the process. Running after what our heart and eyes desire leads us astray. That's why our inner hunger comes with a warning label. Moshe was commanded to inform Israel: "Do not explore after your hearts and after your eyes so that you will be nourished by them."[11]

It's a trap, alright. What our eyes see is what we get. And what our heart seeks, we shall find. It's a self-fulfilling prophecy! The moment we stick our paws into the honeypot, we are seized by its sweet-smelling aroma. And after tasting a bit of its syrupy honey, our thirst is quenched. We feel nourished by it, but only for a fleeting moment.

Moshe is telling us that once caught in the honeytrap, we feel satiated. Why else would we keep coming back? We return for another taste because it actually works. It's reliable. If we want it—and we go for it—we'll surely be sustained by it. Hashem loves us each like an only child. Whatever we request, and however unhealthy it may be, He'll grant it to us. We've always got our hand on the family trust.

It's so easy to get stuck in our Antagonist's trap. It knows exactly how to attract us. It exploits our strongest appetites. And it always knows how to lure us back. Once caught with our hand in the cookie jar, we become dizzy-eyed and lose focus on what's truly important in life. The honeytrap may be nourishing, but it's really just a bunch of empty calories. When addicted to its confections, we're bound to feel even more empty and lost without them.

Like a wandering bear, we'll be seen stomping into every confectionary store looking for just a little lick while on our way to nowhere.

TAKEAWAYS

- When the hungry bear takes hold, our only concern is to fill the empty hole.
- Latching on to externals just means we're trying to extend our territory, our personal domain.
- We have an inner hunger to connect to something much greater than ourselves.
- Our Antagonist sugarcoats everything.

---

11. *Bamidbar* 15:39.

- Doing acts of kindness for others satisfies our need for attachment.
- What our heart seeks, we shall find. It's a self-fulfilling prophecy!
- Our Antagonist may exploit our strongest appetites, but all we get from them are empty calories.

Chapter 11

Eye Candy

Are you unable to pass a candy store without entering? When you walk past the store, and your heart starts to flutter, that's when you know that your eyes must have been seized by the eye candy openly displayed in the window.

That thinking is very much in line with Yehudah ben Teima. To protect our heart from filling with desire, we have to be looking ahead, from a bird's-eye view. When we're hyper-focused on our eyes, we can then guard our heart in turn, preventing us from dancing right into the intriguing store.

I'm not sure if Yehudah ben Teima ever walked past a Cinnabon restaurant, but we all know their secret. They've been pumping their sweet sugary-cinnamon smells out into the malls for years. The whole point is to excite us into prancing up to the counter to buy their legendary made-from-scratch tasty cinnamon rolls.

When Moshe counseled us not to explore outside of ourselves, it was because he knew that looking toward externals would cause us to go astray. He did this by alerting us to the honeyed desires that exist within our hearts. And for him, our eyes come in a close second. Moshe wanted to emphasize that once your heart has been struck by desire, if you pursue it, the next thing you know you'll be munching on a yummy sugary bun. It's an easy theorem: You desire it, you see it, you eat it.

When we want something badly enough, we'll do everything in our power to get it. If we get a whiff of it, we might even be willing to roam an entire mall in order to discover it.

Yehudah ben Teima must have also known about this phenomenon. He knows we all wrestle with an inner hunger. Suffice it to say, he has more faith in us than we may imagine. If our heart becomes excited from a sweet smell, he trusts that we'll decide to avert our eyes, and not to seek that which we desire.

You know what'll happen if we do. We'll find it! And when we see it, we'll roll right into Cinnabon's legendary honeytrap.

It's impossible to know what initially triggers the craving. It could be a smell or a thought that brings to mind a fond memory, or a sight in a shop window that catches our eye. Either way, it's your heart that tells you, "You've gotta have it."

Back in World War II, when my dad was in the US Navy, they had a mantra for the mess hall: "Take what you want but eat all you take." We've all put too much food on our plates at one time or another. "I can't finish it all," we declare. That's when we can always count on somebody to quip, "I guess your eyes were much bigger than your stomach."

INSATIABLE

When we've overfilled our plate, it can be quite embarrassing. We feel guilty. We've been working so hard to curb our cravings, and yet we realize that this time we overdid it. It's easy to judge ourselves too harshly. But do we stop to think who's really doing the judging?

Many people prefer to just wallow in their errors. It's much easier to feel down and get sad about our mistakes. The problem is that sadness leads to laziness. You know you're pretty far gone when you start to relish in it. Feeding these negative and unhealthy messages is a clever way to permit ourselves to continue feeling down. It's the perfect excuse. And if we keep at it, over time, we probably won't even recall what life was like without them. It's hard to imagine that anyone could be so dedicated to this negative behavior, but truth be told, we forget why we started to relish it in the first place.

COMPLACENCE

Laziness is sticky. It leads to being *complacent*. No matter how little we try, we still won't be totally satiated. But it doesn't really matter anymore. It just seems easier to wade around in our lowliness. At least, it's something we can be sure of.

I know it's difficult to shake these negative messages. Deep down, we just want to let them go and stride forward. My heart goes out to all of the people stuck in this muddy middle. It's like they've met their match, and they've decided that there's no longer any point in trying.

It doesn't help that when we're in a really low place, our efforts to climb out are always met with opposition. It's defeating. When we feel at a loss, our Antagonist is compelled to repeat its message: "You might as well just go for it. No matter what you do, it won't be enough. You'll still be deficient and incomplete anyhow."

A BRAND-NEW ROUTINE

This is the nature of a bad routine. Like a wandering bear, we continue to pursue that which we expect will fulfill us. We press on because we hope that it will free us from our emptiness and the pains of hunger that pang from deep within. A bad routine takes off the edge. When we gulp down that next drink, smoke that next cigarette, or swallow that next bite, it'll suffice, but the relief will only be short-lived. We won't really be satiated—at least not for the long-term.

We become accustomed to our bad habits. They become the status quo, and as we indicated before, it's hard to change routine.

King David spells out for us a clever way to start anew and leave those old routines behind. Instead of continuing to feed our hungry bear with garbage, he directs us as to how to become a much more upstanding person. Hashem loves us. Whatever we want He'll give to us. When we start to seek that which is in our best interests, He'll help us find it and achieve it. King David indicates that when we endeavor to do something good for ourselves or a friend, Hashem will help us see it to completion. Feeding our hunger with something healthy and positive makes us the wiser for it.

Instead of filling ourselves up with the bad, we now satiate our appetites with the good, and as King Shlomo relates, "An upstanding person eats to satisfy their soul, but the belly of the wicked will feel hungry [i.e., lacking]."[1]

When things are amiss, and we start to look for the good in everyone and everything, each bite of goodness will start rebuilding for us a brand-new routine. The old status quo will become passé. King Shlomo suggests that this new habit of doing acts of kindness is a worthy routine to adopt. It's the best way to curb our appetite. In time, we may transform ourselves into becoming real *menschen* and, as he repeatedly promises, "Hashem will never starve the soul of the upstanding person."[2]

TAKEAWAYS

- When we're hyper-focused on our eyes, we may in turn guard our heart, preventing us from dancing right into our Antagonist's trap.
- It's easy to judge ourselves too harshly when we've given in to our cravings.
- When something catches our eyes, it's our heart that tells us: "You've gotta have it."
- Once caught in the honeytrap, we feel satiated, but only for a fleeting moment.
- When in a low place, our efforts to climb out are met with opposition.
- Doing acts of kindness curbs your appetite, and in time, you'll have transformed yourself into becoming a real mensch.

---

1. *Mishlei* 13:25.
2. Ibid., 10:3.

Chapter 12

Mighty as a Lion

ROARING OUTA BED

How do you wake up in the morning? Every morning Hashem grants us a brand-new opportunity. He retrofits us with new clarity and imbues our heart with the courage to tackle our newly updated world. We're like a new creation, and the whole world has been placed fully into our hands. And just like the profound sense of gratitude that Leah felt when Yehudah was born, before we even roll out of bed, we verbally thank Hashem for kindly rebooting our soul.

This bud of gratitude is what speaks to the wisdom in our heart, awakening a spiritual hunger and permitting us to serve Hashem with all of our might. It's no wonder that Rabbi Yosef Caro, while following the same structure as the *Tur*, opens his code of law with the words: "A person should be mighty like a lion to stand up in the morning to serve their Creator."

You were created for today! You've been imbued with a lionheart. Your perception has been refreshed from the moment that you awoke. You're positively hungry and super stoked to take on the day.

COMMITMENT

The path is now cleared before us. Clarity is compared to knowing, but as G.I. Joe always remarked, "Knowing is only half the battle." We've taken heed and our heart is now unfettered, but in order to truly seize the day, we must still take the lead. True commitment starts from within the chambers of our hearts. In order to realize our greatest potential, our hearts need thoughtful direction and guidance from the outset. If not, they'll be left to their own natural devices.

> *The heart has its beaches, its homeland and thoughts of its own. Wake now, discover that you are the song that the morning brings, but the heart has its seasons, its evenings and songs of its own.*[1]

The heart is the pivotal place from which we commit to either go down a good path or a bad one. Life is about choices, and making the right choice is what activates and actualizes the wisdom in our hearts.

The material for life's choices is the information that we hold dear: what we value, feel right about, and heartfully intuit. You know what's best for you within the depths of your heart.

KING OF THE BEASTS

The morning is the most opportune time to take command of the day. Taking the lead demands that after sharing our morning gratitude, we immediately don our royal crown. And as we know going into this, being a leader of this capacity means we're apt to receive a ton of opposition. We must therefore wear our crown wisely.

Hashem crowned you as the King of the Beasts!

Wise leaders approach the day by leaning on their right foot and with their hearts pointed in the right direction. When we roar out of bed with the right get-up-and-go, our day is bound to be filled with positive energy. We will be awe-inspired and filled with the motivation necessary

---

1.   Robert Hunter, "Eyes of the World," on *The Wake of the Flood*, 1973.

to accomplish our daily tasks from the get-go. It's the lionhearted who live life to the fullest.

As we've already established, leaving our heart to its own tricks isn't the wise way to go. It leads to making mistakes, and with every stumble, we're prone to increase the emptiness that exists within our hearts. It's this additional schmutz that takes away from our efforts to pursue our goals for the day. The Antagonist takes advantage of this oversight, pipes in, and makes every effort to take control with every fumble. It does this by encouraging inauthentic thoughts to arise from the empty space in our heart, seizing our mind and corrupting our vision. These distorted thoughts are what prompt mishaps and cause mistakes to happen.

To the untrained eye, our Antagonist's foreign ideas seem incredibly authentic, and we are therefore bound to make improper life decisions. When we do, we'll be stuck walking the Antagonist's path and not our own.

How do we regain control of our heart? The Antagonist has wrapped its muddy fingers around our thoughts, and our heart has succumbed to its whims. The odds are that our hearts have become severely jaded in the process. But, in line with Yehudah ben Teima, we've already been entrusted with the wherewithal to break ourselves free. We do this by engaging with our internal wisdom.

Our aim is a shift in perspective, and in order to initiate this process, we must leave our old and corrupted thoughts behind. And that demands a heartfelt moment of mourning for the initial misemployment of the wisdom in our heart. According to the prophet Yirmiyahu, we achieve this by speaking directly to our heart, describing how infuriated and embittered we are at its undoing. This inspires our heart to beseech Hashem, as the verse states: "Their heart cried out to Hashem"[2]—the heart itself will discuss with Hashem the deep regret we have for our ill-directed behavior.

---

2. *Eichah* 2:18.

The very effort of reaching out to Hashem is what unshackles the heart. It quiets the mind, allowing us to take pause to reflect and redirect. Once relieved from our Antagonist's burden, we may start thinking clearly and guide our heart to make better choices in life all over again.

POWER OF CHOICE

Rabbi Akiva didn't get too caught up in the subject of free will. He knew that Hashem watches us closely, and yet at the same time, allows us to choose our own destiny. He was even known to say, "Everything is foreseen, yet the freedom to choose is given."[3] The power to choose is our greatness. Our future lies in our own hands. We govern our actions, and they're to our credit alone.

When we put into motion our *power of choice*, our personal story goes into full swing. Taking a stand allows us to live independently, and our ability to choose between good and bad grants us the means to forge and maintain our own path. As leaders, we get to choose our own direction, and we determine "who" we will be from this day forward. The power is in our hands to choose to either become lofty or lowly, as Rabbi Yechiel Michel Tucazinsky points out in his book, *Gesher Hachaim*:

> *Man can choose his path between these extremes. He can degrade himself to the lowest of all levels or else raise himself aloft to encompass the entire world. Should he wish, he can become a cruel, venomous beast of prey...He has the capacity to become an angel on high.*[4]

It is ultimately a choice between life and death. The wrong decision leaves us with nothing, but the right one permits us to truly come into our own: "This free mastery of himself molds man, and either gives life to himself or else destroys and reduces it to nothing."[5]

---

3.   *Pirkei Avos* 3:15.
4.   *Yeshayahu* 47:8,10 and *Tzefaniah* 2:15, quoted in *Gesher Hachaim*, pp. 75–76.
5.   *Gesher Hachaim*, p. 82.

As we mentioned before, Hashem said, "You shall choose life!"[6] And as Ben Azai said, "The reward for doing a mitzvah is a mitzvah."[7] We may infer from this that we reap what we sow. The future is in our hands, and Hashem doesn't place in our hands the bad or the good, but choice alone. After we've chosen the path that's most fitting for us, we reap the benefits. When our first step is in the right direction, we can count on Hashem to join us for the ride. And with every good step, Hashem helps us to continue to stride on the good path.

At the end of the creation narrative, Hashem's Torah resolutely states: "And Hashem saw all that He had done, and behold it was good."[8] Yet, with all of this goodness, it still wasn't a finished product. There was still more to do. As we walk in Hashem's ways, we take the lead in completing His project. We add more goodness to the world every step of the way. Hashem created a world filled with goodness, but so much has been hidden and rests only in potential. It is our duty to actualize it.

A big part of growing up is learning to discover and realize our underdeveloped goodness. We are the ones who make it good, and it's our job to make good on the good. As Rabbi Tucazinsky puts it, it's upon you to "make your own good."[9]

TAKEAWAYS

- Every morning Hashem provides us with new clarity and gives our heart the courage to tackle our newly updated world.
- Gratitude is what speaks to the wisdom in our heart, awakening a spiritual hunger and permitting us to serve Hashem with all our might.
- The heart is the pivotal place from which we commit to either go down a good path or a bad one.
- The Antagonist encourages inauthentic thoughts to rise from the space in our heart, seizing our mind and corrupting our vision.

---

6. *Devarim* 20:19.
7. *Pirkei Avos* 4:2.
8. *Bereishis* 1:31.
9. *Gesher Hachaim*, p. 85.

- Hashem watches us closely, and yet at the same time, allows us to choose our own destiny.
- It's upon you to make good on the good, or as Rabbi Tucazinsky puts it, it's upon you to "make your own good."

Chapter 13

Decisions

Why are decisions so darn difficult to make?

We can attribute our decision-making struggles to a normal case of FOMO (fear of missing out). It's like we're all prophets when it comes to decision making. Just toying with the idea of making a choice unboxes the sense that once we clop down the gavel, single out an idea, and select one option over another, we're certain to die of regret. That's because our Antagonist places in our hearts the overblown idea that making a decision means we're automatically excluding all the other options. This is why we often feel like we're losing out on something really important. All it takes is one decision, and somehow, we've already missed out, and it all happens so quickly.

LOSS OF POSSIBILITY

Our humanity is struck when confronted with choosing only one style of car, one job, one school, one idea, or one person with whom to spend the rest of our life. What if we only had one story to tell? How about only one path to walk?

We all feel constricted when confronted with our own finiteness. It's uncomfortable. We become anxious and scared. It feels restrictive. Decisions become weighty. We've even felt our breath start to shorten at times. Any choice that we make immediately cuts us off from any other possibility. Once we choose one thing, there's no more "other."

Every other option has vanished. The potential loss is frighteningly overwhelming.

We've only begun the decision-making process, and we've already found ourselves mourning the *loss of possibility*.

BLACK OR WHITE

Life isn't always so black or white. It's much grayer than some of us would like to admit. When it comes to life, it's a lot easier to adopt a more extreme approach. Taking our Antagonist's more reactive, outside-in approach just seems simpler. That way we can at least define ourselves by who or what we think we're *not*. It comes with less responsibility.

Approaching decisions from the inside-out demands more elbow grease. It requires that we already know what we're packing: our personal strengths and what we truly value.

In order to make an educated decision in life, we need to begin from a solid sense of self. The world out there may be fuzzy at times, but in order to make a long-lasting decision, our intentions must be crystal clear. It may not be just black or white yonder, but our decision-making process must certainly be.

Making a decision requires that we choose one thing over another. And in order to be solid about forging ahead, our attitude must truly be an "all-or-nothing"!

Why do we often balk at making such concrete decisions? Maybe it's because we don't want to view ourselves as children. It's belittling. A kid's world is much simpler. All little ones perceive things as black or white. Youngsters do better with boundaries. Contrary to the common teenage bravado, they actually yearn for limits and rules.

Making a commitment, however, means taking a stance—and putting up boundaries feels like a bold move. It all sounds so inflexible, but when making decisions, people somehow feel guilty about relating to the world as if it's only black or white. It doesn't help that our Antagonist sweeps in and murmurs, "Don't limit yourself. Don't be so married to that idea. Why are you so committed to that job? Life is way too short to be devoted to only one person."

The next thing we know, we begin to regret our decision. We hem and haw. Then our imagination kicks in and laments, "Look at all the possibilities I could have had. If only I would have chosen the green over the red. Or maybe I should have just decided to wait on it."

Does that sound like a solid commitment to you? It's like a person who's still living in the past. One moment, they're making a choice, and then minutes or days later, they're grasping and yearning to take back what they believe they've lost in the process.

Do you mourn the loss of gray? The regret that seeps in after making a decision only muddies our thoughts. It creates a pain in our heart and our neck, and throws us deep into doubt. We get stuck in its muddy middle. The existential tension that arises leads us to start questioning who we are and how we define ourselves. This confusion is due to our soft attempt at making a concrete, long-term, black-or-white decision.

Authentic, longstanding decisions are forward-thinking. Until we make a full-on choice, we're stuck just going with the flow. There's something about swinging the gavel that makes it sound final and complete, but in fact, the opposite is true. Limits put up walls, but they also open doorways. Viewing our decisions as all-or-nothing is the trick to unlocking the gateways to our greatest potential.

EDUCATED DECISIONS

I'm not suggesting that we jump into anything; it's important to make educated decisions. Everyone is entitled to do their own research and receive professional advice. Listening to others share their own experiences can be very enlightening; we can learn from others who have gone down the very same path before us.

It's good to approach new beginnings in an educated way. It's impossible to predict what the future holds, so a wise person allows themselves a trial period when starting a new career, entering a new relationship, or even when committing to a new diet. This is sticky business because our Antagonist will wake up and undoubtedly try to fill us with doubt before we fully commit. When it succeeds, we're likely to get anxious after two meetings or a week in the new office, or to even cheat on our diet before seeing any real results.

Do you always stick to the personal commitments you make in Elul? That's why the trial period also needs to be black or white. Each step forward should be delineated, and the trial period should also contain very clear rules and conditions. We get to decide how much time to dedicate to each established period. Making thought-out and well-planned decisions gives us the freedom to script the narrative for ourselves, and we can always stop and reevaluate things once we've reached our goal.

What do decisions have to do with being locked into a negative behavior or thought pattern? Decision-making can be contraindicated. What about showing favorites? The drug addict prefers his particular spice over another. The gastronome loves her special delights. We don't dare to ask, "Why do you limit yourself?" and suggest, "If you knew where to look, I'm sure you could find other good drugs as well."

There's always another option. Wise decisions set up healthy boundaries. They're like guardrails that provide us with a straight shot as we walk along our own path. Without them, it's hard to maintain trajectory.

BLINDERS

Putting up blinders isn't the best for every situation, but when it comes to making good on our decisions, it's a wise way to go. There's nothing more enjoyable than having a sense of clarity in life. Life's decisions are like that. Wearing ethereal blinders puts other potential options at bay. Although the road is often shadowed by many shades of gray, we still need to cut through the haze. The sharper our choices, the clearer our path.

Do you have a difficult time sticking to your commitments? If so, you haven't truly committed yourself to carrying out the task. That's what commitment means. There must always be follow-through. It's not enough to just pledge our devotion to carrying it out. We must execute it. We've got to stick to it.

STICK TO IT

My father was an avid ballplayer when he was young. Although his last job was in business and budget administration, based on his high school counselor's advice, he began his teaching career in Detroit Public

Schools as a physical education teacher. Like most suburban kids in America, we had a basketball net affixed to the roof of the garage. One day, my dad grabbed the ball, took me outside to the driveway, and said, "Son, today, I'm going to teach you about the world!"

This was sort of a play on words because the game we proceeded to play was called "Around the World." He directed me to stand underneath the basket, and although he hadn't played in decades, to my surprise he made every shot—nothing but net. As he proceeded to travel the driveway and describe the world, he bent his knees, held the ball between his eyes, and shot with his arm fully extended. The ball seemed to drop effortlessly by his self-professed perfect form.

Every time he stepped into position, he illuminated the three components necessary to succeed in this world. With every shot he repeated, "Number one, be persistent. Number two, be consistent. And number three, be sure to always follow through."

He put an extra emphasis on the follow-through. He coached, "Always make sure to watch your hand go into the basket." As the ball soared through the air, he arched his hand, visualizing its descent into the basket, and in with a swish went every ball.

Sticking to commitments doesn't mean that we can't ever change our mind. We just have to first put the plan into motion, as there's no better way to find out if it was a good decision or not. We can always reevaluate and switch to a different path at a later date. It takes experience to make wise decisions. Through trial and error, we get the knack of it, and with a proper amount of persistence and consistency, we become models for what it means to carry things through—to make good on our life's choices.

Every decision must be made with an all-or-nothing attitude. And when we stumble and fall along the way, it's this particular attitude that makes it much easier to get up, brush ourselves off, and recommit to carrying out our decided task. Each time we pull ourselves up by our own britches, it builds confidence. Every fall holds the potential for a new beginning. It's an opportunity to regather ourselves, take aim, and walk our path as the person we've been striving to be.

TAKEAWAYS

- One decision and we're already mourning the *loss of possibility*.
- Life is often fuzzy and gray, but clear decisions start off with an *all-or-nothing* attitude.
- Limits put up walls, but they also open doorways.
- Educated decisions set up healthy boundaries, acting like guardrails that help us to maintain trajectory as we walk down our own path.
- Not sticking to our commitments means that we didn't truly commit to carrying out the task in the first place.
- A wise person sticks to their path by being persistent and consistent and by visualizing themselves on the follow-through.

Chapter 14

Bold as a Leopard

STIFF-NECKED

Leopard-like personalities are a force to be reckoned with. They're wily. They're known to be "high energy." They're troublemakers. When they run amuck, they tear their prey down. When they attack, they suppress. They leave others feeling caught in a pickle. The way to handle this sourly stiff-necked character is to match their toughness, to also be as hard as metal.

According to the midrash, Daniel's vision of the four beastlike creatures that emerge from the watery depths is referring to the four exiles that the Jewish people would endure over the centuries. Quoting the midrash, the *Maharal* paints both the Babylonians and the Greeks as being brazenly unrefined, rocklike personalities.

- The Babylonians are described as decked in silver and gold, and the Greeks clad in iron. The midrash illustrates Nebuchadnezzar, the king of Babylonia, as bearing a coat of copper. This bothers the *Maharal* because the prophet Daniel didn't witness a leopard-like creature until the third beast surfaced from the ocean's depths.[1]

---

1. *Ner Mitzvah*, pp. 16–17; *Daniel* 7:6.

- The Greeks are often compared to Daniel's third, leopard-like beast. But peering into his vision we do see him describing the brass armor of Babylonia as having their "belly and thighs made of copper."[2]

The *Maharal* admits that the leopard is undoubtedly as brazen as copper, and to help the idea along, the beast was also sporting something even more bold and audacious—Daniel's lion-like, yet human-like, creature was fitted with "wings of an eagle."[3]

It takes a winged, shameless beast to fly to every corner of the earth with full intention to conquer it.

TOO BASHFUL

A non-brazen person seeks relaxation and contentment. Humble, modest, or timid people can too easily become complacent. Often, they just don't have enough gumption to spring into action. They're not the first to jump at an idea, run after an opportunity, or join in on a worldwide movement. Brazen people are on fire! They're compared to *aish*, and fire is always ablaze. It doesn't settle. It's not interested in sitting to chill. It's always on the move, stays eager, and is fully adrenalized. Fire is pumped, winged, and well-armored.

According to the midrash, Alexander the Great also spread his four wings wide. This brazen king of the Greeks would not sleep a wink until the entire world was suppressed under his wings. Like a bird shooting in every direction, he refused to relent until all his brashness was exhausted. Greece saw itself as everything—the only thing. It sought to trample everything else in its path. How could it allow anything else to exist?

The *Maharal* compares this characteristic to the last and nastiest creature that Daniel envisioned. It was caught gnashing its fierce, ironclad teeth from the start. Nothing was safe from its iron jaws. The Greeks pulverized everything with their steel. They treated everyone as a pariah. They preyed on the poor. They clung grossly to anything

---

2. *Daniel* 2:32.
3. Ibid., 7:4.

inconsistent and lacking. In the end, no rickety wall or faulty foundation was left standing.

STOUTHEARTED

Yehudah ben Teima taught us to be mighty, powerful, and leopard-like. This hard-wearing personality trait can be used for the good or for the bad. You can motivate it either to go against your grain, or to hold yourself tight to your path. When you're bold as a leopard, nothing can deter you from staying true to yourself.

How can we be sure to do the wise thing? According to the *Tur*, Yehudah ben Teima demands that we remain unabashed in the face of our Antagonist's opposition. He doesn't expect us to attack our Antagonist head-on but believes that we're wise enough to stay one step ahead of its game. We can avoid it altogether. We just have to arouse the wisdom that's hardwired in our heart. When confronted by a hostile environment, we can maintain our trajectory by tapping into and leveraging our cardiac output. And we do so by speaking to our heart.

Yehudah ben Teima trusts that we know in our heart of hearts what is truly in our best interests. When we get a sense of being under fire, speaking to our heart will trigger a natural repulsion to the haze of the smoke screen our Antagonist has blown in our direction. This gives our heart enough pause to set up a proper roadblock, guarding us from stepping away from the path that continues before us.

As wise people, we must be able to keep our wits even in the face of opposition. This level of equanimity requires that we always have our whereabouts in check.

Are you able to imagine drawing a line between yourself and your Antagonist? If you struggle at this, there's still a way to cleverly employ the resources hidden in the chambers of your heart. Like we said, in line with King David, the path toward becoming a wise person is to become a clever one.

The way to become wise in a clever way is by educating our heart. Every time we manage to get unstuck, regain our balance, and find solid ground, we are allotted an amazing opportunity. We don't just learn more about our Antagonist's nefarious ways, but we also refine our *power of distinction*. This power allows us to gain more clarity about which paths are good for us and which ones are sorely not.

Every time we succeed at climbing out of the quagmire, it creates a certain degree of muscle memory. Whether we're fully aware of it or not, we've been educating our heart all along about the perils we face at the hands of our Antagonist. Now we're aware of this, and once our enlightened heart has become wiser to our Antagonist's tomfoolery, we're given direct access to this learned cardiac wisdom.

It takes a lot of grit to turn our eyes away from our Antagonist's influence. But once we do, we're free to move forward. We become unshakable, unstoppable, and unapologetic. This stouthearted attitude is enough to remind our heart to tap into its natural resources. It palpitates, awakens itself to the danger, and unleashes its natural repulsion to our Antagonist's false-hearted demands.

HARDWIRED FOR IT

In other words, Yehudah ben Teima entrusts us with the duty to show great chutzpah in the face of adversity. In times of necessity, it shouldn't be difficult to muster up boldness and brazenness, for it's a part of the very fabric of our being. The huge mishap of the Golden Calf gives testimony to this. We actually created a new entity in opposition to Hashem. And this stubborn attribute continues to course through our veins. We have a knack for it!

Reish Lakish indicates that three traits of brazenness were gifted to Israel. They are the very tools that allow us to guard, maintain, and regain control over ourselves. It's like we're on fire. It takes a *stubborn, stiff-necked*, and *obstinate* personality to block out our Antagonist's radically imposing agenda.[4] This bullheaded personality is indispensable. It's what makes us unyielding to our Antagonist's whims and keeps us right on track and still on the go. Like a four-winged creature, our Antagonist yearns to take away our freedom.

The more unshakable we are in the face of persecution, the sharper are our efforts toward living more wisely.

---

4. *Ner Mitzvah*, p. 12.

PURSUIT OF WISDOM

We are built to be wise. As carriers of this leopard-like trait, we've been designed to develop a keen, mindful power of discernment, and to be able to enact good judgment. We must be shrewd in order to acquire wisdom. This also helps us maintain an unapologetic attitude.

It's important to keep in mind, however, that when we doubt ourselves or fear the expectations of others, this ability is withheld from us.

The bombastic words of a brazen person may be toxic to those who speak them, but with proper intention, they may also be used to arouse, excite, motivate, inspire, and inflame oneself to learn and to pursue wisdom.

How did Hillel become such a big scholar? He listened to his own wise words: "A bashful person can't learn!"[5] Rabbi Meir once asked the question, "Why was the Torah given to Israel?" He answered with wit, "Because they're absolutely brazen."[6]

How else could we have received Hashem's Torah? The light of His Torah is known to set things ablaze. Just before Moshe died, he recounted that the fiery Torah was given as a blessing to B'nei Yisrael, saying, "The Lord came from Sinai and shone forth from Seir to them; He appeared from Mount Paran and came with some of the holy myriads; from His right hand was a fiery law for them."[7]

Rabbi Yishmael's son describes Hashem's Torah as a blazing inferno. To properly receive it, we have to match it. We must also be on fire.

TAKEAWAYS

- The way to handle a stiff-necked character is to match his toughness.
- Brazen people are on fire! They don't settle.

---

5. *Pirkei Avos* 2:5.
6. *Beitzah* 25b.
7. *Devarim* 33:2.

- When we arouse our wise cardiac output by speaking to our heart, it sets up a proper roadblock, guarding us from stepping away from the path that continues before us.
- Climbing out of the quagmire creates a certain degree of muscle memory, educating our heart about the perils that we face at the hands of our Antagonist.
- It takes a stubborn, stiff-necked, and obstinate personality to block out our Antagonist's radically imposing agenda.
- The words of a brazen person are often toxic to the one who speaks them, but with proper intention, they may be used to arouse, excite, motivate, inspire, and inflame oneself to learn and to pursue wisdom.

Chapter 15

By Invitation Only

One day, my dad and I went for a walk, and we passed a private lawn that had a sign bearing the words, *Keep Off the Grass*. My dad looked at me with discerning eyes and challenged me, "Son, do you know the reason why they put up that sign?"

"Uh...so people won't walk on the grass and destroy it," I sheepishly replied.

"No. Because somebody once walked on their grass," he resolved wisely.

THE INVITE

> *Hashem canvassed Kayin, "Why are you bothered? Why are you looking so down? If you do what's good, won't it raise your outlook? But if you don't do what's good, wrongdoing crouches at the door; and it desires you—but you should master it."*[1]

Rava maintains that our Antagonist first appears at our doorway as a wayfarer. It then cleverly masks itself as a guest, but by the third visit, it somehow manages to transform itself into the master of our house.[2]

How does it get into our home in the first place? We invite it in. It only gains leverage over us if we open the door and wave it in.

---

1. *Bereishis* 4:6–7.
2. *Sukkah* 52b.

Maybe it would be prudent to hang a shingle on the door that reads, *Antagonists Keep Out!*

When we find ourselves in conflict with our Antagonist, and that old negative behavior or thought pattern starts knocking us about, it's because we invited it in. It's like we decided that our Antagonist deserves a more prominent role in our life than we do. And worse, we've really taken it to heart.

Inviting our Antagonist into our heart is tantamount to setting it a place at our dinner table. Surprise! Now we look over and it's sitting in our living room. The next thing we know, we're rubbing arms with it on the couch. This should start to make us feel a bit uncomfortable, and that's a good thing. When we don't enjoy its presence, next time we might think *not* to invite it in.

Invite it in? Do you remember hearing the knock at the door? Do you remember unlatching the door and letting it in? How about providing it a vacancy in one of the chambers of your heart? Most people don't recall how it got in. Not letting it in takes practice. Through trial and error, we become wiser to it, but in order to do that, we must first become cleverer about how we perceive it.

The more times we knock heads with the Antagonist, the more attuned we become to its antics. The moment we start to dislike how it imposes itself on us and our life, we may be inspired to take action. We embrace the raw character needed to manage it. Developing a wise attitude toward it demands a certain degree of grit. When it comes back soliciting, the wise person in us looks to the doorway in our mind and trumpets, "Go away! I'm tired of letting you in."

LET IT BE

Hashem told Kayin that if we use something meant for the good in a bad way, our misdeed will follow us home. It perches itself next to our door, obsesses over us, and loiters there until we are able to regain control of it.

Rav Shimshon Raphael Hirsch finds fault with the misconception that has befallen us based on a misunderstanding of the words, "your wrongdoing crouches at the door." He's perturbed by the fact that the word "crouch," or *rovetz* in Hebrew, has been described as an Antagonist who sits in waiting, ready to pounce.[3] He considers the depiction of a wicked wild beast lurking, just waiting to overpower us and drag us into its lair, to be too immature. That's because when probing the usage of the language of *rovetz* in relationship to animals in other places of the Torah, the very opposite appears to be true.

Rav Hirsch claims that there isn't one single instance where an animal that's "crouching" is considered to be "lurking in waiting." On the contrary, the beast always appears to be unconcerned and is peacefully resting. In line with this, our Antagonist may perch itself at our door, but it has no intention of hassling, tormenting, or assaulting us in any way; it's too busy napping.

But it is clearly not in hibernation. We are told that it "desires you." You've stumbled and whet its appetite, and now it craves to be with you; it's hungry for you. Rav Hirsch suggests that when we look to see how Hashem treats the language of *teshukah*, desire, in other parts of His Torah, it depicts a type of devotion or longing for love.

King Shlomo's famous words are a prime example. When speaking of one's greatest love, he sings endearingly, "I am my beloved's, and his desire (*teshukaso*) is for me."[4] And looking back at the first documented human relationship, Rav Hirsch paints the picture of a loving wife who finds the completion of herself in her devotion to her husband: "And to your husband will be your desire (*teshukaseich*)."[5]

That's why it is so difficult to shake our Antagonist. It is completely devoted to us, enamored by us, and longs to be fulfilled by us. It is "head over heels" in love with us. It's in everyone's best interests to allow it to serve us.

However tumultuous a relationship it may be, we're practically married to it. When we're not fulfilling our spousal role, our Antagonist turns the tide and judges us unfavorably. It reacts by holding its love back from us. It pokes us, pulls our chain, and tries to convince us to

---

3. *Hirsch Commentary on the Torah* (Feldheim, 1966), pp. 102–103.
4. *Shir Hashirim* 7:11.
5. *Hirsch Commentary on the Torah*, p. 84.

become the person it wants us to be. When we find ourselves experiencing this degree of *gevurah* (power), it's a surefire way to know that we've appointed our Antagonist as master over us.

COUNTERATTACK

What happens when our greatest concerns take over? What occurs when our self-doubt, anxiousness, obsessions, and blindness start to flow inward? Our *power of preservation* awakens. And now we're poised and ready for the counterattack. This means that we are stuck in a reactive mode.

Amid all this commotion, we lose our whereabouts. We feel vulnerable. We're caught in fight-or-flight mode. And if we end up in a fight, who will be doing the attacking, and who will be attacked? It's all on us, that's who! And there's no real love in self-harm.

All our Antagonist wants is for us to rule over it and to control it. Like Kayin, Hashem trusts we will able to turn this bad situation into a good one. But until we're ready to just leave it snoozing at our door, we're more apt to invite its influence into our life. Rav Hirsch indicates that our Antagonist longs for us to "regulate it, rule over it, and direct it." That is the Antagonist's calling in life.

Rav Hirsch clarifies this, stating, "By you mastering and guiding it, it achieves its purpose, and that's why it longs to achieve it. For there is not a single natural tendency in Humanity which is, in itself, either good or bad."[6]

The Antagonist too wants to achieve its purpose in life.

IT AIN'T ALL BAD

Rabbi Chaim Friedlander shares an extraordinary idea in his book, *Mesilos Chaim B'Chinuch.* Other Jewish sources are known to say the following: From the time of birth, our bad nature rules over our good one.[7] Throughout our childhood, our animal-like senses take charge, leveraging all of our thoughts and behaviors. When we develop into

---

6. Ibid., p. 103.
7. *Sanhedrin* 91b.

young adulthood, our good nature begins to blossom, and eventually comes into full play.[8] As we mature over time, with the help of our good side, we're able to rule over the animal that lives within.

Rabbi Friedlander squelches this two-tiered approach by asking a number of poignant questions: If we were born solely and completely bad, how could we ever be held accountable for any of our bad actions? Anything we think or do will inevitably be bad. Furthermore, how could anyone expect us to do anything good? If we are intrinsically bad, from where would we have learned to be good? And what would even inspire us to try?

When annoyed at active kids, people often say the following: "That child is pure *yetzer hara* (bad nature)," and, "He's just a *vilde chayah* (wild animal)." That just seems to explain everything for them. People don't see much harm in having this attitude because they say in their hearts, "In the future, when the child matures, they'll receive their *yetzer tov* (good nature)." And that, too, somehow solves everything; all will be good after that.

Rabbi Friedlander stresses that being born with an active bad nature is likened to being born in sin. Were you born all wrong? He asks, "If you were a born sinner, how could you ever do any good?" If we are pure badness—really bad to the bone—how could anyone teach us to do anything good?

Rabbi Friedlander doesn't leave us hanging. He reveals for us the story of what really happens at birth. He states that people are born with both good and bad natures, and neither is more dominant than the other. As a matter of fact, he implies that they both begin in a state of rest; they're not awake yet. They're not at all animated, and that's because they're made out of what he calls *"chomer gelem."* This is best translated as original raw materials, or what we colloquially refer to as inanimate matter.

Inanimate matter is untapped, closed-off potential. It lacks depth and influence. It's simply not going anywhere. In line with this, when

---

8.   *Avos D'Rabi Nosson*, chap. 16.

children are behaving poorly, we may all agree that they're acting like animals. But they're not doing anything wrong! It's not a sinful act. They may be living a raw and solely physical existence, but their behavior has nothing to do with having an actively bad nature.

The Antagonist is too busy snoozing.

It's inevitable, as we all know, that eventually the badness will wake up. Rabbi Friedlander suggests that between the ages eight and ten, we begin educating children about goodness. As children of prophets, we're able to predict that their good and bad natures will both be big factors in their lives. It's wise to beat it to the punch and take prophylactic measures by teaching them early on how to use the good while leaving the bad behind.

A little kick in the pants: this infers that we, ourselves, already have to be on that level by the time our child turns eight! Kids don't miss a beat. They're hyper-observant. As a reminder, the only reason our Antagonist awakens from its static, raw, and inanimate position is because we water it, feed it, nurture it—and empower it. We wake it up!

Let it stay asleep.

Startling it may even be considered *gezel sheinah* (literally, stealing sleep). The Sages compare this act to causing someone personal pain or injury. Awakening a sleeping bear, in general, doesn't sound very wise. It may be enamored by you, but waking it up is just asking for trouble.

TAKEAWAYS

- When we use something meant for the good in a bad way, our misdeed will follow us home, and if we are not wise, we may even invite it in.
- This wicked beast may appear to be lurking, but in truth, it is unconcerned and is peacefully resting.
- Your Antagonist actually desires you, seeks to be loved and fulfilled by you, and wants to be mastered by you.
- It is important to begin teaching children between eight and ten years old about goodness, because eventually, the badness is going to wake up.

- It's wise to beat it to the punch and take preventative measures by teaching children early on how to use the good while leaving the bad behind.
- The only reason why our Antagonist awakens from its static, raw, and inanimate position is because we wake it up!

Chapter 16

Quick as a Deer

Whether it's our heart or our mind that awakens us to action, it's certainly our legs that propel us toward our destination. According to the *Tur*, Yehudah ben Teima was hinting to us in the end of his Mishnah that being quick and light as a deer refers specifically to our legs. He adds that our legs are vehicles for doing goodness in this world. And thanks to King David, we learn that it's possible to leave the bad in the dust by running toward it. Whether we intend to do an act of kindness, or even something less praiseworthy, our legs carry a full guarantee. They're eager to fulfill whatever it is that we're aspiring to, as Rabbi Yochanan says, "A person's feet are his guarantors; to where he is summoned, there he is led."[1]

The path we wish to take, there we shall be led. Our legs vow to accompany us on the way, as Hillel states: "To the place that I love, there my feet lead me." A person's feet lead him to wherever his heart desires.[2]

LET YOUR LEGS DO THE WALKING

One quick look at our bodies, and we can see that our feet are the furthest distance from our minds. When stuck in a rut, leveraging our *power of distinction* is no longer an option. That's because in order to get

---

1. *Sukkah* 53a.
2. Ibid.

ourselves moving, our thoughts must first be channeled through the heart. And let's face it: if we're currently in a sticky situation, it means that both our heart and ability to make proper decisions have already been compromised.

We're steeped in the muddy middle. It's stressful, and we're finally getting fed up with being stuck in our Antagonist's trap. We're inspired to seek a way out. What's our first step? How do we remove ourselves from its clutches? How do we begin to stride forward?

In line with King David, speaking to our legs is our only way to jump-start our heart. And like the story of the famous do-gooder and great Inspector Gadget, we may lean over and cleverly command our feet, "Go, Go, Gadget Legs!" Once our body is mobile and our blood starts to pump, our heart is free to do the right thing.

As the *Sefer Hachinuch* asserts, "Hearts are drawn after actions."[3] Once our legs are mobile, the wisdom in our heart resuscitates, and we feel fully alive. Thanks to our legs, we're able to guide our heart right back on track.

TAKEAWAYS

- Our heart or our mind may awaken us to action, but it's our legs that propel us toward our destination.
- Running toward goodness leaves the bad in the dust.
- The path in which we wish to take, our legs vow to take us there.
- When stuck in our Antagonist's trap, speaking to our legs is our only way to jumpstart our heart.
- Once our body is moving, the wisdom in our heart resuscitates, and then our legs guide us back on track.

---

3. *Yalkut Shimoni* 147.

Chapter 17

Do, Then Listen

*Rabban Gamliel's son, Shimon, would say: I have
grown up among the Sages, and I haven't found
anything better for the body than silence. Study isn't
the essential, but action is key.*[1]

FEET FIRST

T he emphasis King David places on his legs indicates that for
him, actions speak louder than words. When we're feeling
anxious, ignoble, or especially paralyzed, it's difficult to regain composure. Our Antagonist has seized our mind, and any attempt
to verbalize our intent is bound to go awry. Before we think to open our
lips, it's best to first take a moment of silence, a second just to quiet
our minds.

All of a sudden, our Antagonist will be tricked into thinking that
we're someone else. Our silence pulls the wool over its eyes. Its anten-
nas are thrown off, and it's tricked into reading us as a wise person.
King Shlomo strengthens this insight, revealing, "Even a fool will be

---

1.   *Pirkei Avos* 1:17.

thought to be wise if silent; when he seals his lips [he will be considered] understanding."[2]

But if we do foolishly open our lips, we're most likely to "let it all hang out." We'll begin to overflow with negativity. And we start mimicking the critical and defeatist messages that our Antagonist often delivers, recounting its story and not our own.

> *It's better to remain silent and be thought a fool than to open one's mouth and remove all doubt.*[3]

A word to the wise: airing our thoughts may even be hazardous to our health, because they have the power to unlock our internal gates to the Antagonist itself. Once our heart is open, the Antagonist is free to come in, sniff around, and make itself at home. It listens to our tone. It hears us hinting: "Don't worry. I'm still with you. You're still the one calling the shots."

There are times when silence trumps transparency. When our Antagonist becomes too much to bear, it's helpful to remove ourselves from view. Once it can't find us, we may quiet our mind. We may slow down our breathing and place all of our thinking aside.

Once we've accomplished that, we regain the ability to reset our compass. Then we may start off walking in our desired direction. As we walk to our new destination, we may now safely revise, rescript, and verbalize our narrative in a more positive light.

SHAKE A LEG

When stuck in the muddy middle, it behooves us to toughen up, form a stiff upper lip, and let our legs do all the talking. Once we shake a leg, we're instantly unstuck, and we're free again to talk our walk. This was one of the revelations we experienced at Har Sinai. We were so thirsty for Hashem's Torah that we were willing to embrace it all. We didn't

---

2. *Mishlei* 17:28.
3. Maurice Switzer, *Mrs. Goose, Her Book*, originally published in 1907.

even give it a second thought. We jumped at the opportunity, saying, "*Naaseh v'nishma*—We will do and we will listen."[4]

This "do, then listen" approach to life can be scary. It requires a sink-or-swim attitude. This school of thought happens to be a common business model. After boldly jumping into a position, only then do we start to learn the ropes—and we pick up the basics afterward. This is how many people have jump-started their careers. You may be thinking that jumping in feet first is what got us into this sticky mess in the first place. I'm simply proposing that we leverage the same businesslike skill to spring ourselves back into action.

Leaping forward is the most courageous way to get our legs moving and free ourselves from our Antagonist's grip. When feeling paralyzed and stuck in a seemingly never-ending negative pattern, it's often necessary to take such an extreme leap of faith. While living in the *olam ha'maaseh*, the world of action, we sometimes find this clever business model to be our only recourse. It's what permits us to take leaps and bounds. It lifts us off the ground, shifts our vantage point, and affords us a new perspective.

Once on the move, we can show the world that we really mean business. We can be a model for what it means to be lionhearted in the face of adversity. With our legs in full swing, we may talk our walk. It's this step forward that gives us the ability to teach others the ropes. Although it's scary not knowing what may lie ahead, shaking a leg places us in a good position to show others how to leap beyond the face of the unknown.

FEAR OF THE UNKNOWN

Unlike Hashem, we don't know what the future holds. Acting without thinking may sound highly irresponsible, but at times, it's the only practical solution. New waters must be breached, and that may require taking a significant leap. I'm not suggesting acting blindly. And if you do decide to jump, you're certainly not alone. It wouldn't be the first time in history that someone willingly vaulted over the iron wall of the unknown.

---

4.   *Shemos* 24:7.

Not every leap forward leads to instant success. We need to be realistic about how we set our goals. It's the small actions that help us to move forward in life. Leaping into the future may seem like a huge endeavor to us, but in reality, we're only just inching forward. Moving a hairsbreadth ahead is really our aim.

There's purpose to attacking life with leaps and bounds. It's not only a clever way to get unstuck, but it also manages to launch our true selves into the future. Any attempt to hurl yourself out from the muddy middle deserves to be celebrated.

Overcoming the *fear of the unknown* is a big part of our legacy. With one fell swoop, B'nei Yisrael announced that they would "do, then listen." We let our legs do the talking. We leaped to the task at hand, broadcasting a willingness to both deliver what Hashem was stipulating for us in the moment, and also listen to whatever He might ask from us in the future.

GET A JUMP ON

Yehudah ben Teima believes that before we head out on our journey, it's wise to be prepared. Wise people keep a keen eye on the path ahead, and plan for any potential problems that may arise in the future. Like Yehudah ben Teima suggests, while soaring above, we may see what lies ahead with a bird's-eye view.

Life can often be quite unpredictable. It's hard to know what might be awaiting us around the bend. Getting an early jump on things permits us to avoid getting caught in our Antagonist's trap. Rabbi Moshe Chaim Luzzatto, known by the acronym of his name, *Ramchal*, reflects upon this in the sixth chapter of his work *Mesilas Yesharim*. Like Yehudah ben Teima, he proposes that it's wise not to give our Antagonist the reins, and that requires not allowing it to get muddled up in our actions from the get-go.

If we give the Antagonist an inch, it takes a mile. It just weighs us down. As the *Mesilas Yesharim* explains, we sense the burden even more because our nature is already extremely heavy. We're made from earth and water, and these are very weighty materials. No wonder it's so difficult to get oneself up and running in the morning! It's hard to take on new challenges when our own physicality is weighing us down.

In order to leap forward, we have to go against our own nature. Continuing to play a heavy hand won't lead us to success. But with the right amount of enthusiasm, we can give ourselves the lift necessary to get a jump on life. According to the *Ramchal*, we may uplift our feet by doing good deeds. Doing acts of kindness permits us to rise above our material nature. This, in turn, affords us an amazing amount of *chizuk* (strength). Acts of kindness empower us, giving us just the boost needed to progress forward.[5]

When we're not sure what lies ahead, we can tap into the endless pool of emotional wisdom and spiritual encouragement that's already been allotted to us. Furthermore, we're not expected to do this all on our own. When we reach such an impasse, we may picture ourselves standing before the Jordan River, ready to cross with the Jewish People into the Land of Israel. When feeling hesitant to cross, we may invite ourselves to step right into Yehoshua Bin Nun's wet sandals and imagine what it would be like to receive *chizuk* directly from Hashem: "Did I not instruct you to be strong and to have courage, and to not fear and be dismayed, for Hashem is with you wherever you go."[6]

SHPILKES

I was quick, and I did not delay keeping your commandments.[7]

A good dose of *shpilkes* helps a person continue forward.[8] Impatience may not be the most flattering personality trait, but there's a benefit to having a few "ants in the pants." It's important to do whatever it takes to keep moving on. I'm not suggesting a fast-paced, all-in-the-rat-race style of movement. It's much better for a person to sustain a low level of *shpilkes* and keep our agitation on a low burner. As we indicated

---

5. *Berachos* 32b.
6. *Yehoshua* 1:9.
7. *Tehillim* 119:60.
8. *Shpilkes* is a Yiddish word that literally means "sewing pins," and is used to refer to nervous energy, as in "sitting on *shpilkes*."

before, we're never really stagnant; we're always in a state of transition. We're either moving forward or slipping back. It's in our best interests to always be moving toward greater spiritual heights.

When do we finally get to stop moving? In short, when we're buried in the ground. Now is not the time to stop. Stagnation kills. And anyone who's had a bout with paralysis knows exactly what I mean. It's not fun feeling forever stuck in the muddy middle.

The old-school way of pulling ourselves out of a rut, according to Akavia ben Mahalalel, is to have our minds enter into a conversation with our soul. Our Sages would enlist their spiritual side to give their body an essential boost by recalling:

> *Know from where you came, where you are going, and before Whom you are destined to give a judgment and accounting. From where did you come? From a putrid drop. Where are you going? To a place of dust, maggots, and worms. Before whom are you destined to give a judgment and accounting? Before the King of kings, the Holy One, blessed is He.*[9]

If that doesn't give you *shpilkes*...

A person who is no longer living has obtained whatever spiritual level they may reach in this world. The Talmud teaches that we bless the living, "to go in *shalom* (peace)," as a person moves toward greater spiritual heights. That's because we care about the process, and one should find peace along the path they are walking.

We bless the departed, "to go to *shalom*," while recounting the amount of spiritual achievement they earned in their physical life. That way, we may place the focus on their final destination. And we hope that the address at which they arrive will be a peaceful one.[10]

Our physical existence is what allows us to transform and perfect ourselves. We do this through our achievements and by always making sure to stay on the move. Death and stagnation are big downers. It's no

---

9. *Pirkei Avos* 3:1.
10. *Mo'ed Katan* 28a.

surprise that those who are stuck deep in the muddy middle tend to lose vitality. They're stuck lamenting the loss of life.

The Sages maintain that focusing on death has the power to jump-start our heart. They believe that mourning the loss of our worldly opportunity to stride forward should be enough to do the trick. If this works for you, great! In the next chapter, with a simple twist in perspective, I begin to advocate a much more peaceful, self-empowering, and uplifting solution.

TAKEAWAYS

- Actions speak louder than words.
- When feeling stuck in a seemingly never-ending negative pattern, we may jump ourselves into a new position; by shifting our vantage point, we can afford ourselves a new perspective.
- Overcoming the fear of the unknown is a part of our legacy.
- Doing acts of kindness helps us rise above our own nature, giving us just the boost we need to progress forward.
- Maintaining a low level of *shpilkes*, impatience, helps us to continue striding ahead.

Chapter 18

Run Away

Run away from your problems!

At the risk of getting myself in hot water, I humor myself for being the first therapist to tell people that in order to move ahead, you actually have to run away from your problems! It's clever advice, too, and I know this because that's what King David suggests. In order to seek *shalom* in life, he says, first, "Remove yourself from bad."[1]

And by just taking a cursory look at his life, what do you imagine King David did every time he found himself in a sticky situation? He ran away. In order to avoid getting further entangled into his problems, he would run as far away from them as he possibly could:

- In David's younger years, King Shaul sought to put him to death. Yonasan went to talk him out of it and encouraged David to go run and hide, warning, "Shaul, my father, seeks to put you to death, and now, protect yourself now in the morning, and you shall remain in secret, and hide."[2]
- While David was playing music, a terrible idea fell upon King Shaul, and he made a lunge at David with his spear. This was good reason for young David to skedaddle: "[David] slipped away

1. *Tehillim* 34:15.
2. *Shmuel I* 19:2.

from before Shaul, and Shaul drove the spear into the wall, but David fled and escaped that night."[3]

- King Shaul sent messengers to David's house to watch over him and put him to death in the morning. "And Michal, his wife, told David, saying, 'If you don't flee for your life tonight, tomorrow you'll be put to death!'"[4] He slipped out the window: "And [he] went, and fled, and escaped."[5]

- King Shaul found fault with Michal for letting David escape: "Now David had fled and escaped, and he came to Shmuel..."[6]

- Achimelech the Kohen gave David some sacred bread and armed him with Golias's sword, and David fled to Adullum.[7]

- The people of Keila said they'd give David into King Shaul's hands, and away David ran.[8]

- His fate lying in the hands of King Shaul, David decided to seek refuge in the land of the Philistines: "And David arose. And he and the six hundred men who were with him, crossed over to Achish..."[9]

- Avshalom declared his rebellion, and David uprooted his servants: "Arise and let us flee; for there will be no escape from us before Avshalom. Go quickly lest he hurry and overtake us, and bring evil upon us, and smite the city by the blade of the sword."[10]

When we stick around, our Antagonist joins us in the struggle. It puts on the pressure. All the while, it sings Macbeth's witches' song: "Double, double toil and trouble; Fire burn and cauldron bubble." And like the famous response of Harry S. Truman: "If you can't stand the heat, get out of the kitchen!" This is precisely what King David is asking us to do.

---

3. Ibid., 19:10.
4. Ibid., 19:11.
5. Ibid., 19:12.
6. Ibid., 19:18.
7. Ibid., 22:1.
8. Ibid., 23:13.
9. Ibid., 27:2.
10. *Shmuel II* 15:14.

He wants us to take his lead and to quickly find for ourselves a more secure place to be.

Splitting from the scene is usually all that's needed, but our Antagonist has been cleverly watching all of our moves. In order to keep moving on, we must gather a few more tricks under our belts to avoid its convincing rhetoric. When stuck in the muddy middle, the trick is not only to run away; it's also important to know exactly where we are headed.

DANGER ZONE

Leaving our bad situation in haste may be the best move to get out of our Antagonist's clutches, but if we haven't already planned our new destination, we're most likely to jump feet first into the *danger zone*. However unhealthy our Antagonist's whims, we've grown used to its rules and expectations. At some point, we adopted its negative messages and ideas as if they were our very own. Now that they're deeply ingrained in us, they've become a part of our basic framework, acting as our beacon. They've become our normal.

In other words, embracing unhealthy externals leaves us stuck living under a set of foreign rules and world order. This outside-in approach is certain to award us with a very sticky, reliable, and secure position in our Antagonist's domain. On its own, running away isn't always a sure thing. Stepping out of our Antagonist's grip could actually place us in jeopardy. In truth, removing ourselves from any ordered environment places us straight into a world cloaked in chaos. Without any plan, we're bound to step right into the void.

We witnessed the impact of this chaos being played out in full force at the onset of the establishment of the new Lithuanian-style yeshivos in Europe. Before the yeshiva boom and the opening of Volozhin Yeshiva in the early 1800s, there were only a few hundred Talmudic students. They were scattered in private study halls throughout Europe.

The flood of students flowing into the yeshivos was a sign of great spiritual energy and influence pouring down onto the world from above. Although the halls were now rumbling with excitement, this intellectual and spiritual power that sparked Jewish learning was also received by others, but in a very different and negative way. It was the juice that inspired the development of the Haskalah (Enlightenment) movement. This movement not only reignited Hebrew for secular purposes, but it worked hard to establish a cultural and moral renewal devoid of Hashem's Torah.

The world was rampant with spiritual energy, and during the transition from one learning framework to the other, many Jews were lost to the Enlightenment.[11]

Why is this all so interesting? As long as we're plugged into a working framework, it's relatively easy to stay strong. It's the transitional space between A and B that's proven to be quite precarious.

Once we've left our current situation, we eventually merit to find solid ground, but unless we've established our next destination from the start, we're most likely to leap straight into the *danger zone*.

Before we head out on our journey, it's worth our time and effort to decide where we'd like to direct our spiritual creative energy. It may demand life experience, but like King David, it's always in our best interests to plan our destination.

EYES ON THE PRIZE

> But one's desire is in Hashem's Torah...And whatever he does will succeed.[12]

King David's solution to this problem is clear. He indicates that Hashem's Torah is our address, and as long as we keep it at the forefront of our mind, we'll continue to walk the straight path and our legs will be compelled to move us in the right direction. And if we happen to stumble, we can get back on track by reminding ourselves of what's important, meaningful, and valuable in our lives. This isn't new; we've been inspired before. We've all run after something we considered important at one point or another. Perhaps it was something good and kind we did for somebody else. We know that works. And this is because we're interested in looking out for other people's best interests as well.

---

11. *Nefesh Hachaim*, gate 1, commentary by Rabbi Yisrael Eliyahu Weintraub.
12. *Tehillim* 1:2–3.

If you're just starting off, heed the following warning: Anything we set our sights on will work. It will take our mind off our situation and permit us to take on new strides. Earthly pleasures also briefly shift us out of our Antagonist's focus, but they simply aren't good enough for the long run. Not everything is as dependable as Hashem's Torah.

But doing kind deeds is nothing to shake a stick at. They help hold our world together. As one of the last surviving members of the Great Assembly, Shimon HaTzaddik said, "The world stands upon three things: upon Torah, upon Divine service, and upon acts of kindness."[13] Doing whatever is in our power to get our legs moving upholds this last pillar. Yehudah ben Teima's deer is built for doing acts of kindness. Doing something positive for another person is the quickest route to reignite the wisdom in our hearts. Once it is awakened, our eyes will be better focused on the prize.

Remember King David's theorem? He would first focus on his legs, then his heart, and then his eyes. We may see success by following the same clever design. Hashem's mitzvos keep us on trajectory, and once our legs are up and running, as King David divulges, "The statutes [pathways] of Hashem are uplifting, gladdening the heart—Hashem's commands are clear, enlightening the eyes."[14]

When we're walking the straight and narrow, the flames in our hearts burn stronger. We see things much more clearly, and this helps to keep our eyes directly on the prize. And we get help from above along the way. In a tight spot? Just shake a leg! And Hashem will fan the warmth in your heart, sit shotgun, and tag along with you for the ride.

We learn this from Yaakov Avinu, who "raised up his feet" to travel to the east.[15] It was heartwarming, and the trek easier going, once he'd heard the good news that Hashem was going to accompany him for the journey: "Yaakov's heart lifted his legs and it became easy for him to walk onward."[16]

---

13. *Pirkei Avos* 1:2.
14. *Tehillim* 19:9.
15. *Bereishis* 29:1.
16. *Bereishis Rabbah*, 70:8, *Rashi*.

NACHAS RUACH

The Vilna Gaon indicates that every action that we do has the amazing capacity to draw down vital energy from above.[17] This vitality is meant to help us do more good things. Although it imbues us with great inspiration, he stresses that this particular energy isn't remotely comfortable. It doesn't sit quietly. It gives us a good dose of the *shpilkes*, putting on the pressure until we're encouraged to act again. And it doesn't stop nudging us until we've received the right amount of pleasure earmarked for doing it.

We can conclude from this that whether this descending energy is good or bad, when we actually see things through, we always receive a bit of *nachas ruach*, comfort, in the end. That's how the Gaon explains Ben Azai's statement: "A mitzvah causes another mitzvah, and a negative act affords another negative act." Whether our action is good or bad, we will always receive some degree of satisfaction in the end.

The greater our misdeed, the greater the negative energy that descends, adding more flames to our desire to do it again. But this is also true for good things. Our acts of kindness invite good energy to cascade from above, inspiring us to do more positive acts for ourselves and for others. And that's rather satisfying!

FLEE FROM MISDEEDS

It's difficult to hide from our mistakes. Wrongdoing works like a boomerang: what goes around comes around. Bad actions always come back to their original source.[18]

But what if we were to implement our power of return? The boomerang is scheduled to swing back to the very point of its release. One step in the direction of home, and we've cleverly left that spot uninhabited. We simply won't be there when the boomerang returns.

What happens if we only *think* about throwing the boomerang? The Talmud states that contemplating a misdeed is worse than actually

---

17. The Vilna Gaon's commentary on *Mishlei* 1:23.
18. *Rambam, Pirkei Avos* 4:2.

committing it.[19] Even the vibrations of our thoughts can make an impact. They, too, somehow leave an indelible impression.

The issue is that it is our thoughts that eventually lead us to action. In line with Yehudah ben Teima, a wise person knows that when a thought floats up into the mind, it is still within one's grasp, still in his control. If the boomerang has not yet been released, then there's no real need to sidestep it. Our best recourse is to drop it and run.

But that particular thought is going to follow us wherever we go unless we've already set in place a well-planned destination. The solution that Ben Azai provides for this in the beginning of his Mishnah is key: "Run to pursue a minor mitzvah and flee from a misdeed."[20] Running to do what may appear to be even a trivial mitzvah leaves our misdeeds in the dust.

TAKEAWAYS

- In order to seek *shalom*, you must "remove yourself from bad."
- Unless we've established our destination from the start, we're most likely to leap straight into the *danger zone*.
- Hashem's Torah is our address, and as long as we keep it at the forefront of our mind, we'll continue to walk the straight path, and our legs will be compelled to move us in the right direction.
- Our acts of kindness invite good energy to cascade from above, inspiring us to do more positive acts for ourselves and for others.
- A wise person knows that when a thought floats up into the mind, it's still within our grasp to drop it and run.

19. *Yoma* 29a.
20. *Pirkei Avos* 4:2.

Chapter 19

Run Toward Yourself

*Akavia ben Mahalalel would say: Reflect upon these
three things and you won't come into the hands of
wrongdoing. Know from where you came, to where you
are going, and before Whom you are destined to give a
judgment and accounting.*[1]

When we leave an uncomfortable situation in a hurry,
what we're actually accomplishing is twofold:

- On one leg, we're uprooting ourselves from our current
position and leaving all of our Antagonist's negative odds and
ends behind.
- On the other foot, we're already heading to a new address which
offers us hope for a brand-new beginning.

This affords us the opportunity to leave our false sense of self in the
dust while looking for a new and improved authentic version. Hashem
was intending this very thing when he gave the directive to Avraham
Avinu of "*Lech lecha!*" With one fell swoop, Hashem told Avraham to
both "go to yourself!" and "leave yourself behind!"[2]

---

1. *Pirkei Avos* 3:1.
2. *Bereishis* 12:1.

It's not easy to pick oneself up and walk away from everything. It's also a bit harsh to be asked to scrap our old home for a new one. Think of all the people and memories we'd be leaving behind. And who's to say we're not going to run into our Antagonist along the way? It would be beneficial if we had a map that would keep us on track, successfully point us out of the city, and unswervingly guide us toward our desired destination.

We have varying degrees of emotional attachment to the different places in which we've resided. When headed out on a spiritual journey, in order to slowly peel oneself away from familiar locales, it's helpful to review the wise steps that Hashem laid down for Avraham Avinu upon his own exit.

In order for Avraham to go find himself, he was first told to leave his country of origin, then his birthplace—the city he grew up in—and lastly, to step out of the door of his father's house. It's a bit mind-boggling that Hashem appears to have flipped around the normal order of things. I'd have thought that starting out on one's journey would first require removing oneself from one's parents' home, rather than exiting the country. Maybe there are plenty of other hot spots in your hometown that you'd like to try first. Maybe it would be just as well to start off close to home. But if our life's task is to become the father or mother of an entire nation, or say, the whole world, maybe we'd require an even greater disconnect.

Or maybe the message is much simpler. Anytime we want to migrate to a new place, it's best to make sure it is better suited to the person we are striving to be. By laying out these specific instructions to Avraham, Hashem is directing us as to how we should approach change in our lives:

- Leaving "your land" suggests that before we move to another place, we should first check to see if we can relate to the history of the people and their country.
- Leaving "your birthplace" suggests evaluating what we may have in common with the people and their culture.
- Leaving "your father's house" suggests choosing a town in which to live that fits the "new person" we aim to become.

Once we've accomplished that, it's much easier to go find a comfortable new home for ourselves and our loved ones. But before I lead you on a wild-goose chase, it's important to note that Hashem's real intention for Avraham was to go find his true purpose in life. Sometimes, we have to step outside of our current selves in order to achieve this. Although separating oneself from one's friends and family is not normally recommended, for those who need to totally upend their mindset, they may require taking serious action. In order for them to succeed, they may have to pick themselves up and physically leave the home in which they were reared.

Either way, the journey requires that we make some sort of significant move. Hashem is simply trying to illustrate that making a shift affects us on many emotional levels. The emotional ties we have for our country are less entrenched than those we have for our province. We have a slightly deeper connection to our region and have a greater attachment to the city in which we were raised. In short, the closer to home we are, the tighter the feelings and the more difficult it is to create a disconnect. When running away to find our true selves, it's not easy to leave our old familiar selves behind. Are you headed out to go find yourself any time soon?

WHEREVER YOU GO, THERE YOU'LL BE

It's best to hold your horses. Before we divorce ourselves from the situation that we're fleeing, it's important to make sure we can confidently say that we have fully invested ourselves in our current place. If we haven't wholly tried, we're most likely going to trip over the same old challenges that our Antagonist will provide for us in the future. The Antagonist will also be there when we arrive. Not only will it meet us at the door, but we'll most likely come onto the scene feeling free and off the hook, only to open our bags and realize that we actually brought all of our struggles and concerns along for the ride.

GREENER PASTURES

It's not easy bein' green.[3]

It's not unusual for people to tumble into the grass-is-greener syndrome. When we're feeling deficient, down, anxious, or confused in our current place, it's common to want to cast our eyes on the behaviors of others. This may even lead us to covet what they have. The grass starts to look greener on their side.

I work with a number of young people who dream about dropping out of school in order to get a job. Not just any job; they want to get a great big job, one that promises to make them millions. Although they're young and have very little life experience, they feel that their current "employment" leaves much to be desired and are quick to gravitate to what society stipulates as "real"—total success. Any sort of highfalutin dream would work better for them than having to remain in their current predicament. It doesn't seem to matter how supportive their school or parents are trying to be or if they don't already feel themselves to be like a million bucks. They've somehow learned to manage their time by staring out the window at the nice green pastures across the street.

They don't realize that it isn't any easier being green. If they're really going to be a big-shot businessperson someday, wouldn't it be more reassuring to achieve big-shot student status today? Being a student is their current gig. Success now promises success later. An instituted habit of failure now will most likely lead to failure later.

CHANGE YOUR MAZAL

Mazal comes from the Hebrew word *nazel*, fluidity. If you have a runny nose, you have *nozelet*. If you're suffering from a leaky hose, your nozzle has probably come loose. The events that we experience in life are connected to a higher flow. Through the *mazalos*, the fiery spheres

---

3.   Joe Raposo, "It's Not Easy Bein' Green," originally performed by Jim Henson as Kermit the Frog on *Sesame Street* and *The Muppet Show*.

and stars that radiate from above, Hashem impacts and guides us as we walk our own path. He behaves as our beacon. He pours His great influence down upon us, supporting us in all of our endeavors. He uses this fluid energy to help us complete our daily tasks.

The great big balls of fire in the sky represent our relationship with destiny. Not only were they briefly in a fixed alignment when we were born, but we're even capable of tapping into their creative energies today. This is how we draw down Hashem's influence with every life decision.

It's common to wish a hearty *mazal tov* to our friends and family when congratulations are in order. On a joyous occasion, it's as if we're saying, "Congrats! And may you have a stellar day!" What we truly hope to convey is, "May your celestial bodies be in the perfect arrangement for you to receive everything that you need in order to fulfill your task for today!"

Our relationship to our *mazal* impacts us both physically and spiritually. It has the potential to both fill our cups with wisdom and line our pockets with riches. We learn from a teaching in the *Talmud Yerushalmi*, "Change your place, change your *mazal*,"[4] that changing our location is so powerful that it has the capacity to realign our *mazal*.

Some even say that we can change our *mazal* by redirecting our thoughts and actions. Making efforts to be the person we truly want to be is what changes our *mazal* for the better. The Sages also say that we can enact change by having an open dialogue with Hashem and extending our goodwill to others. The more we strive to be who we truly are, the more specific the tools that we need to pack for the journey.

It's normal to beseech Hashem when we feel as if something's lacking. Another word for deficiency is "poor," and that's what inspired Rabbi Yonasan to say, "Whoever fulfills the Torah in poverty will ultimately fulfill it in wealth."[5] The greater our efforts to grow more into our authenticity, the more we merit to receive higher help. Starting off poor and simple leads us to receive the treasures necessary to stay on track.

---

4. *Shabbos* 6:9.
5. *Pirkei Avos* 4:9.

Our *mazal* echoes as we stride forward. At the speed of light, our actions travel heavenward. The light then descends, reflecting from on high. As we flow onward, Hashem bursts with love, overflowing and broadening our portion in the world.

But there's also an opinion that says that you can't change your *mazal*. If that's true, don't fret; we still have recourse. We can actually rise above it. With acts of *chessed*, kind deeds, Avraham Avinu was able to distance himself and float above his own *mazal*. That's why we consider him to be greater than Noach who, despite being the most upstanding character in his generation, was still unable to rise above his own destiny. Avraham Avinu, however, was able to go beyond the normal call of duty.

The *mazalos* were given the job of controlling the physical world. But we can free ourselves from them. Since Hashem lifted Avraham above his *mazal*, Rabbi Yochanan maintains, *"Ein mazal l'Yisrael*—There is no *mazal* for Israel."[6] When we walk our path, live according to our values, and fulfill our purpose in this world, we may alter the course of our *mazal*. We're placed right back into the arms of Hashem, and it's only He who guides us.

People who live in accordance with their *mazal* are predestined to play out a certain role. This responsibility may have a myriad of implications. Leveraging it to our advantage really comes down to how we play our cards. It's possible that traveling from one space to another, moving from one job to the next, or entering a new relationship is the very shift one needs to improve their current position in life.

CHANGE YOUR PLACE

Any place to which we attach ourselves becomes a receptacle for the inflow of our *mazal*. It's not always true that the satellites above track us wherever we go. We need to be solidly grounded in order to capture their full influence.

In order to understand this concept, we need to take a peek at how we conduct ourselves at mealtime. What's considered proper etiquette at the table? When we sit down to eat a meal, there's a certain degree

---

6. *Shabbos* 156a, *Rashi* explains that through prayer and personal merit, we may alter our *mazal*.

of continuity, unity, and connection to the place in which we've decided to sit and dine. Normally, we thank Hashem at the end of the meal by *bentching*—blessing Him kindly and profusely for the tasty morsels He provided. If we happen to decide to change our place, get up, and forget to *bentch*, we're required to return to wherever we began eating in order to say our thanks.

This is because we're still attached to the place. We're fully united and committed to being in that space. If we walk away and start a new meal in a brand-new location, we're even required to make a new blessing once we arrive. If our plan from the start is to eat our meal en route, and we intend to *bentch* at a different location, we're obviously not interested in grounding ourselves in the place where we initially broke our bread. Instead, we're fully committed to showing up at our future destination. By intending to *bentch* in a different place, we project ourselves forward in time, uniting ourselves with this new location. The opportunity to thank Hashem only materializes when we've physically arrived.

Yet, if we're already committed to our present space, and for whatever reason distanced ourselves from it, we're bound to experience a loss. When we get up to leave, our relationship to the space suffers, and we're likely to lose touch with our own whereabouts. If so, we've lost our power of distinction, and there's no point in returning to *bentch* in that location. We simply won't be able to find our whereabouts again until we've stumbled upon ourselves sitting at another set table.

TAKEAWAYS

- Hashem told Avraham to both "Go to yourself!" and "Leave yourself behind!"
- If we haven't fully invested ourselves in the place from which we're fleeing, we're most likely to trip over the same old challenges upon our arrival.
- It isn't any easier being green.
- When we're feeling deficient, down, anxious, or confused in our current situation, it's easy to fall into the trap of casting our eyes on the behaviors of others.

- We may change our *mazal* by having an open dialogue with Hashem and being kind to others.
- When we walk our own path, live according to our values, and fulfill our purpose in this world, the *mazalos* relinquish their control over us, placing us right into the arms of Hashem, and it's only He who guides us.

Chapter 20

Bare Bones

Hashem's Torah is perfectly whole, returning the soul;
Hashem's Testimony [His Torah] is reliable, making the
simpleton wise.[1]

KEEP IT SIMPLE

We're the ones who complicate things. Striding forward requires putting one foot in front of the other—one step at a time. Baby steps allow us to accomplish one thing at a time. It's just not possible to take on all of our struggles at once. The way to really start gaining traction is by keeping life simple.

In other words, it's time to downsize. That doesn't require throwing away our worldly goods; rather, we need to focus upon fewer things. This is a wise move, as King David indicates above: to become a wise person, we must start off wholly simple. Be the *simpleton*!

Keeping things simple is the cleverest way to become wiser. Every simple step we take along our way brings joy to our hearts and sharpens

---

1.   *Tehillim* 19:8.

our lenses. Keeping life straightforward and uncomplicated is what allows us to see things for what they truly are.

STAY RELEVANT

In today's world, Jews tend to treat mitzvos differently than in the past.

It could be due to the vast amount of new mitzvah opportunities that have arisen thanks to our return home to the Land of Israel. It's like we're always itching for something new and refreshing to do. Maybe it's representative of the digital, quick-click, access-everything-online generation. Whatever the reason, people want things to be fresh and novel today.

There was once a time when people preferred a simpler life. They even approached the performance of mitzvos more simplistically. Maybe it lacks the luster of today, but people were once more inclined to take the mitzvos that they were already doing and just try to do them better. They'd take their same old mitzvos and make an attempt to reawaken them. Making our mitzvos more vibrant requires performing them with a little more forethought, added feelings of greater purpose, and a bit more focused attention on Hashem.

One example is the extra scrutiny that people place on the first paragraph in *bentching*. This is probably due to it being a specific Torah obligation, making it the most essential blessing of them all. It may have a lot to do with the fact that Moshe penned the paragraph in gratitude to the *mann* that Hashem gifted B'nei Yisrael while traveling through the desert.

Similar to taking upon ourselves a *kabbalah,* a resolution we adopt for the new year—but actually sticking to it—we can give thanks to Hashem by deciding to *bentch* with more clarity this year. I'm not suggesting taking on the whole thing, but as we said, often it's enough to put all of our emphasis on the first paragraph.

If this is still too much, we can join the individuals who have decided to limit their scope by just adding a bit more intention to their Shabbos *bentching*. We'll find that centralizing our energies even once a week is a wise thing to do.

People who try this report, "I'm spending a little more time on it and trying to focus on each word." The point is really to stop rushing. Pay attention! It's best to go over each word with a fine-tooth comb and, to borrow an idea from the *Mishnah Berurah*, to count each word as if we were counting coins.[2] Alternatively, we can choose a different area to focus on, such as acknowledging and giving thanks to the people we encounter throughout the day, or making an effort to give compliments to our loved ones and to focus on their positive attributes. There's nothing more practical than taking something that we're already doing well and just trying to make it better one step at a time. All the complicated stuff will then naturally fall by the wayside.

THE SIMPLE RECIPE

> *He lays up sound wisdom for the upright, a shield for those who walk in simplicity.[3]*

The *Maharal* writes in his Haggadah that it is crucial to keep the recipe simple.[4] He indicates that the *lechem oni* that we speak about at the beginning of the Pesach Seder is usually referred to as "poor bread" or "simple bread."

The *Maharal* focuses on the spiritual side of matzah. The simple recipe is what makes it truly special. According to his understanding, Hashem refers to it as a poor person's bread with the specific intention to reveal its unique quality of being *nivdal*, meaning "separate" and "different" from the physical world. The recipe is so simple that it can only be considered as ethereal and spiritual in nature.

We left Egypt in haste with the *lechem oni*. That indicates that this particularly flat bread has way more to do with speed and agility than sustenance. Hashem emphasized this by hastening our departure. Some say that we even left in the blink of an eye.

---

2. *Mishnah Berurah, Hilchos Berachos* 51, (laws of *tefillah* and *Baruch She'amar* until *Yishtabach*), 8 (*b'berutzah*).
3. *Mishlei* 2:7.
4. *The Maharal Haggadah* (Horev Publishers, 1993), pp. 57–61.

The matzah ingredients are simple—and simple moves. It is quick and light, and it won't slow us down. It makes us light on our feet. The less we're carrying, the more agile we can be. Adding yeast to the dough is a normal part of bread making. Yeast causes it to become elastic and airy, and it's what blows it up. If we let the dough rest and ignore it, it will grow even bigger. According to the *Maharal*, yeast is just an unnecessary extra that is liable to weigh us down.

Matzah's recipe is simple, "poor." There's freedom in poverty and simplicity. Less is more. And too much extra can be too much of a burden. Life is complicated enough all on its own. Increasing the amount of ingredients adds unnecessary weight. It's not worth feeling so overloaded. That said, it still takes a wise person to avoid getting trapped in our Antagonist's overblown sticky dough.

True freedom comes with simplicity. A free person is nimble. A quick leap and the clever person gets unstuck. It takes a simple mind to emerge from the muddy middle, to stand on one's own two feet, and to continue striding forward. When we've got yeast on the brain, it's time to hone ourselves down to the simple things and start walking on our own path. We accomplish this by focusing our energies on making something we're already good at just a little bit better.

There's simply no reason to change the recipe; adding anything else might just sour the mix.

SIMPLE THERAPY

The couples who come to visit me have often already worked through a long list of therapists. After inquiring about their therapeutic experiences, it becomes clear that there is one large issue that overshadows the others.

Their therapists often suggest new ideas, tools, and additional exercises for them to do at home. Although I believe couples do have the wherewithal to work on their own, the exercises and activities they receive sound far from practical. After a few days or a week, they indicate how hard it is to carry out such tasks. They describe them as burdens and say things like: "It was too much for us," "I didn't get it," or, "We just couldn't get around to doing it."

As if they weren't already suffering enough, they left it up to the experts to advise them to add more to the mix. There's no doubt that therapists mean well. The activities they give to their clients are even called "practical exercises." It does make sense to stir in a bit of something to spice up the relationship. And doing activities together can push a couple to focus on one other. It may even force them to get to know one another again.

Just be aware that outside-in activities, external systems, and new tools aren't always a real plus.

SWEAT THE SMALL STUFF

In Rabbi Shlomo Wolbe's work *Alei Shor*, he implores people to take special care with each and every small action in their lives.[5] He urges: sweat the small stuff, not the big stuff. This idea may require a total mental overhaul.

Rav Wolbe indicates that the people who achieve the most in life are the ones who are willing to be stringent with the easier stuff. This infers that they're more demanding when it comes to the "lighter" mitzvos. In other words, when we treat that which we imagine to be light as if it is heavy, then that's what we put our heart and sweat into. One of the jobs of the mitzvos is to reflect back to us what it is in life that we truly value. Depending on our personalities, some values are easier to actualize than others. The ones calling for greater improvement just happen to be the personal values that we're already more attuned to.

We may gather a lot of information about people by observing how they relate to others. Maybe you know someone who excels at the following positive values:

- Expressing gratitude
- Listening actively
- Showing care
- Being quick to lend a hand
- Helping others

---

5.   Gate 2, sect. 2, chap. 4, pp. 189–190.

People's values tend to shine. When a person acts on a value (whether positive or negative), it appears to outsiders as something that they must really care about. Whether a person was born with a proclivity for a particular attribute or he earned it through years of effort, on the surface it looks like an integral part of their personality. It may even look like it comes to them with ease.

There's no greater investment than focusing on the positive values that we're already good at and just trying to make them better. Since they appear natural to us, they may even seem small in our minds. The very fact that we're conscious of them is a big indicator that they could use a good upgrade. One may say, "But I'm already good at it. I'm already being a kind and giving person. Shouldn't I rather focus on the parts of my personality that I feel are really lacking?" There may be truth to this, but nevertheless, when we start by taking on a brand-new goal rather than improving something we're already good at, we're less likely to succeed.

Note: We are all deficient in certain values. Although it's not practical to make them our current focus, we shouldn't totally ignore them either. Targeting the values that come easier to us actually schleps along the ones that we feel are lacking. Just like one mitzvah contains an element of all the others, our values are all equally intertwined.

What we value may not stand alone, but in order to make real progress, it's essential to focus on only one such value at a time.

Here are a few examples of personal values that people have reported come naturally and easily to them. And although they initially saw them as small in their eyes, lending them a tad more emphasis allowed them to make compelling shifts in their relationships and in their lives:

- Saying thank you
- Asking permission before using someone else's possessions
- Returning phone calls
- Speaking respectfully to parents, teachers, or friends
- Showing up on time for appointments
- Listening intently

Here's what's clever about focusing on the small stuff. When we feel stuck in a rut, the clever way out is to take something that's easy in our lives and decide to work at it just a little bit harder. We've been granted such amazing talents and abilities. We've been imbued with extraordinary gifts and strengths. The trick is to treat them a little more seriously. This is how we move forward in life. We take something that we're already good at and make it a little bit better.

Putting slight pressure on what's already natural and easy for us permits us to grow organically. When we cultivate a small idea in this way, it eventually leads to significant results. We simply can't know what sort of gift or reward might come out of each and every small deed.

Rav Wolbe maintains that "this world, the *world of action*, hangs on small actions."[6] Rav Wolbe proves his point by sharing a healthy example: When complaining about a particular ailment, it's often wise to visit a doctor. We might not go right away, but most people are pretty good about making an appointment when convinced that feelings of pain, anxiousness, and disorientation deserve our full attention. After describing our experience to the doctor, they'll diagnose the problem and prescribe a specific medication to relieve us of our symptoms. The doctor will not write a prescription for the strongest dosage right up front. Instead, they'll start us off with the smallest degree of active ingredients possible.

When we visit the doctor again a few weeks later, our prescription will most probably be reevaluated and, if necessary, the dosage may be increased. With every subsequent visit, the doctor may advise to add just a little bit more (or less) until the condition subsides.

And for those who still prefer to sweat the big stuff, Rav Wolbe exclaims, "If the doctor would have prescribed for you a large dosage at the beginning, it might just have killed you!"

Small positive actions lead to huge shifts in life. All it takes is investing a little bit of ourselves a little bit every day. Change is subtle. When we don't keep things simple, we devote our precious time to unhealthy

---

6.   Gate 2, sect. 2:, chap. 4, p. 189.

and unnecessary exploits. Making what we truly value just a bit better, little by little, deliberately removes us from the sticky depths of the muddy middle.

LESS IS MORE

When it comes to overcoming struggles in life, focusing on what we value isn't the only recourse. Focusing on something that we enjoy doing also does the trick. Finding yourself stuck in the muddy middle, you may ask yourself, "What would I enjoy doing right now?" It's important to seek something life-enriching. Maybe you have a hobby. What's your favorite thing to do? Go and do it! Give yourself permission to nurture yourself.

When we're in a rut and don't see the light at the end of the tunnel, it's time to have compassion and do good to ourselves. All it takes is to do a task that we already enjoy for about five minutes a day (or even one to three minutes, if five sounds like too much)!

What's essential is to choose a set time each day and stick to it. That means that it's still important to follow through even when we're not *feeling it*. Indeed, in order to take strides and cover ground, it's important to apply our power of establishing fixed times to all of our transformational endeavors. As we know, the *Shulchan Aruch* treats our duty to be *kove'a itim l'Torah*, establish set times for Torah study, with the utmost stringency. We're not supposed to skip our scheduled learning time even if we might lose money on account of it.[7]

I'm simply suggesting that we apply this very power—which allows us to master Hashem's Torah—for up to five minutes a day, as a tool to succeed in all walks of life.

CUT OUT BURNOUT

We grow by setting aside specific times for what we enjoy, and by being especially particular about completing the task. This comes with a warning: Don't turn three minutes into an hour. Although we have a very specific plan from the start, stopping at the appointed time is a

---

7. *Shulchan Aruch, Orach Chaim, simanim* 155 and 238.

common struggle for most. It is difficult to set our creative juices aside just as they start to flow. When we find ourselves having trouble putting our project down, a clever solution is to remind ourselves that this is surely a sign that we're no longer creating it; instead, it's creating us.

When we push our three minutes into an hour (or even fifteen minutes), we're less likely to find the inspiration to do even one minute the very next day. That's because we experience something called *burnout*.

Our Antagonist doesn't just kick us when we're down; it also looks to mislead us in times of great inspiration. It knows that we have the capacity to get overloaded with the things in life that bring us much joy and pleasure. It waits around looking for us to get excited and overly wrapped up in our own creative energy and then seeks to push us overboard.

Not placing a limit on our creative flow is just asking for it to topple over. It's hard to achieve anything when our creativity is spilling everywhere. The Antagonist knows us well and nudges us along by coaxing, "I see that you're really enjoying this project. I know you've passed your allotted time, but hey, don't stop! Think about how much more you'd accomplish if you'd just give it a few more minutes."

And to our surprise, the following day, we feel rundown and overworked. The thought of getting back to the project is just too overwhelming. Spreading ourselves thin and spraying our creative energy in all directions simply weakens us. It's what deters us from picking up even a finger the next day.

In order to *cut out burnout*, it's best to stick to our own set times and parameters. A person who's interested in personal growth needs to establish boundaries and limits. It's impossible to succeed when our creative energy lacks a proper container in which to catch the flow.

PRIMARY VS. SECONDARY

Unless we have our fingers on the proper guidebook or know the right person who may guide us along, it's easy to lose track of the primary versus the secondary elements in our lives.

Placing all of our energy into what's secondary doesn't just take away from what's truly important, but it also causes our creative flow to go to waste. It, too, leads to burnout. It's exhausting when our efforts are cultivating the less important things in life.

It's not always clear what should take precedence. That's why it's a real blessing to have someone in life who is able to mirror back to us what really matters. Focusing on what is uniquely primary in our life allows us to accomplish more, and there is no substitute for the feeling we get when we know that our efforts aren't for naught.

Pursuing what's primary in life also makes us lighter on our feet. That's because we're hyper-focused on what actually deserves the center of our attention. Directing our creative energies toward what's secondary just weighs us down.

It's essential to find for ourselves a confidant, a person who's willing to be our advocate. A confidant's job is to reflect back to us what's most vital in our life. There's no greater gift than learning how to pinpoint our own strengths and values, and to figure out with whom and to where to dedicate our energies.

When we're stuck concentrating on what's secondary in our lives, rather than what's primary, a clever solution is to select one primary thing to zero in on. Working to make it better lends us clarity and quickly gets our legs into gear. With a guiding hand, we may pick up our legs and zealously embark on our personal journey.

Lending greater focus to what's primary in life makes living all the easier because it's something we're already slated for. It's something we're good at; it's what we intrinsically value. Imagining it to be better isn't at all farfetched. A small daily investment promises us greater clarity, understanding, and the wherewithal to transform our lives for the better. The more we ponder it and the better we direct it, the more we create a positive overflow.

TAKEAWAYS

- To become a wise person, you must start off wholly simple by being the *simpleton*!
- There's nothing more practical than taking something that we're already good at and just trying to make it better one step at a time.

- Simple moves. It's quick and light, and it won't slow us down.
- Sweat the small stuff, not the big stuff.
- Not placing a limit on our creative flow is just asking for it to spill over.
- Focusing on what's primary in our lives allows us to accomplish more and makes us lighter on our feet.
- With small daily investments we transform our lives for the better, and the better we direct what's primary in life, the more it becomes our positive overflow.

Walk Your Own Path

Chapter 21

Pursuit of Peace

Hillel would say: Be of the disciples of Aharon—a lover of peace, a pursuer of peace.[1]

How does one pursue peace?

Remove yourself from bad and hasten to do good; seek shalom and pursue it.[2]

According to King David, first we remove ourselves from the bad, then we do some good, and then we're free to pursue *shalom*. Our ability to separate the bad from the good is indicative of our capacity to understand one thing from another. This is due to our *power of distinction*. And once we know in our heart of hearts what's best for us, nothing should be able to impede us from running after *shalom*.

The Slonimer Rebbe indicates that in our generation, we should be interpreting King David's words in a particularly refreshing way.[3] The Rebbe's conviction is that removing ourselves from bad is no longer the best course of action; it's just going to lead us further down a bad path.

---

1. *Pirkei Avos* 1:12.
2. *Tehillim* 34:15.
3. *Nesivos Shalom*, vol. 1, lecture 5, p. 126.

149

Negativity can snowball, and the Rebbe was convinced that focusing on the bad will simply cause us to get more entangled in the mess that plagues our minds. King David's intention is to help us free ourselves of the Antagonist's influence, not to hurl us deeper into our negative thoughts and behaviors.

Focusing on the broken parts is human nature. We're built to seek what's lacking and deficient in the world and strive to repair it. In order to change our external world, we first need to begin transforming our internal world. But in line with the Rebbe, it doesn't behoove us to start by investigating the full nature of our problems. Analysis has not only become passé in our time; probing into our greatest concerns is a bad move and should be seriously avoided.

It's not helpful to go over our issues with a fine-tooth comb. When heading out on our journey, it may be important to unpack our greatest concerns, but not for perusal. It's much better just to lighten our step by removing the extra cargo. Dissecting our problems takes time and is a highly engaging activity. There's a whole field of people who earn a living by helping people do this. Although we may learn some very interesting information about ourselves in the process, we're more likely to stumble, start feeling down, fall out of touch, and lose our whereabouts.

There's nothing more frustrating than reaching out to others for help, and instead of being set free from our greatest concerns, we find ourselves sliding deeper into the muddy middle. I spoke for months with a person who had been doing "inner child" work with a renowned Jerusalem therapist. He proved to be a pleasant, coherent, intelligent, and talented young fellow in his mid-twenties. He was very likable.

He divulged to me early on that when he was eight years old, he experienced horrific abuse at the hands of a close family member. And although he had decided to forgive the person for his actions, he was still wrapped up in his old feelings and was diligently trying to repair his own self-image.

His childhood trauma followed him wherever he went. In more stressful times, he lacked confidence and blamed his abuse as the source for all of his self-doubt. This normal, articulate, and happy fellow would return home every other week thoroughly traumatized from his thera-peutic experience. His body would shake and his speech would stammer as he would relate his feelings to me, remarking, "I don't know who I am anymore. I don't know what I'm doing anymore. I'm completely lost!"

Like any good friend, I reflected back to him, saying, "I notice that when you come back from your therapy sessions, you appear to be a complete wreck. Do you think it's really helping you? Are you sure this is the best treatment for you?"

"Oh yes. I'm learning so much about myself," he professed.

I shared with him how it's organically impossible for a guy in his twen-ties to step back into an eight-year-old's brain. "Your memories are too distant. You've had a lifetime of experience. Your brain has grown and developed into an adult mind. You could never think of yourself as a child again. It's physically impossible," I explained.

The therapist was continuously throwing the poor fellow into his ear-liest trauma. Imagine! He was being catapulted into the muddy middle every other week. It pained me, but he showed great fortitude. Trauma builds character, and although he returned as a total *nebach*, he could always figure out on his own how to move on. He learned to utilize his own resources and was forced to discover clever ways to remove himself from every challenging episode. Playing music was his refuge.

An important thing to remember about trauma is that it's cyclical and compounding. When a person who has experienced serious trauma in their past ends up having a traumatic day, both the initial trauma and every subsequent trauma resurfaces, leaving them with a heightened degree of psychological pain.

We're stuck reliving all our traumas in the present moment. When catapulted into a cycle of darkness and confusion, there's simply no room for good therapy to take place. This young man was being asked to step into the lion's den every other week. He was tossed into the dark-ness—into a boiling cauldron of awfulness. All in the name of therapy. Think of the horror. And afterward, he'd come back for a friendly detox and help with licking his wounds. It was just heartbreaking.

The Rebbe's solution is novel. He suggests flipping around King David's instructions, reading instead, "Remove yourself from bad *by way of* doing good." In other words, when we seek to do what's good for ourselves and for others, all the bad stuff will just fall by the wayside.[4] Once we're finally doing what's in our best interests, we're able to take pause, glance back, and wonder, "Where did all that nonsense disappear to?" We may not even recognize what was once our greatest challenge as our own anymore. It will be as if it never existed.

Rabbi Baruch Ashlag says that when people want to remove themselves from the bad, they aren't required to dispose of it on their own. That's because the Sages teach that a person simply can't handle a bad thing on their own. He even goes as far as saying that it is life-threatening! Like the Slonimer Rebbe, Rabbi Ashlag insists that harping on the bad never ends well. The effort we put forth into recognizing how damaging and unhealthy our behavior is may just end our life.

What is his solution? Get out of harm's way! "Remove yourself from the path of the arrow," he says. Once we've stepped out of its way, we're able to recognize the problem for what it truly is. Distancing oneself from the bad calms the mind and catapults us to solid ground. This peace of mind is what helps us to safely discern how it has been damaging us all along.

How do we create this necessary distance? By embracing goodness. Once we're on the good path, the bad will quickly fall away. According to Rabbi Ashlag, this is what King David means by instructing us to *do some good*.[5]

That being said, there are times when being plagued by unwanted thoughts and bad actions is so overwhelming that we just need to get them off our chest. Like the story of the young fellow above, when we find it difficult to see our way through the schmutz, it's high time to find a good friend who's especially good at listening.

And remember, it's you who is presenting your immediate concern. A good friend has no intention to pry or to propel a person deeper into the middle of the muddiness. They want what's best for you, too.

---

4. Ibid.
5. Rabbi Baruch Ashlag, *Pri Chacham Maamarim*, maamar 65, on the verse *"Sur mei'ra v'aseh tov"* (2).

Everyone knows that it's impossible to *pursue shalom* when we're missing a positive outlook.

I'm not saying that speaking about our past is off-limits. There are times when it's essential to share an old story. Sharing a negative story, and feeling understood, is an effective way to start progressing forward. Sometimes we just need to let the negativity out. The wiser we are to it, the quicker we begin to hear the damaging words that we speak. It's important to become deeply attuned to the way that we've been choosing to tell our story. The story that we tell ourselves creates our reality. As long as we continue to accept our Antagonist's unhealthy messages, we continue to do ourselves a great disservice, as its job is to muddle the perception we have of ourselves and the world around us. Changing the script to serve our best interests changes our lives for the better.

Our lives are in our hands, and we get to tell our story the way we've always wanted it to be told.

TAKEAWAYS

- Our ability to separate the bad from the good is indicative of our capacity to understand one thing from another.
- Being hyper-focused on the bad will simply cause us to get even more entangled.
- The goal is to free ourselves of our Antagonist's influence, not to hurl us deeper into our negative thoughts and behaviors.
- Trauma is cyclical and compounding.
- Remove yourself from bad *by way of* doing good.
- When we start to share our negative story and hear the damaging words that we speak, we become more attuned to the way we've been choosing to tell it.
- Changing our story to serve our best interests changes our reality for the better.

Chapter 22

Creating Shalom

I n order to gain strides on conquering our negative thoughts, behaviors, and feelings, we must first create *shalom* with our Antagonist. Before we begin, I'd like to clarify what I mean by asking a question:

What's bothering you?

It's what you're most concerned about. It's what you wake up thinking about in the morning, it's what's gnawing at you throughout the day, and it's what's going through your mind while lying in bed at night. You may even find yourself talking or complaining about it to others.

It's your *overflow*.

Maybe you're feeling anxious or down in the dumps, or you lack impulse control. Are you struggling with making a decision? Are you drowning in emotions and not sure what to do with them? Maybe you're sensing that life just isn't going as planned. Whatever it is that's bothering you right now, put it into writing. It's best to open a Word document or find a notebook in order to jot things down for the following exercise. While you're doing that, have in mind the following four guiding principles:

1. **Choose one!** You may be overwhelmed by a number of issues right now. Zero in on one of them. Maybe even pick the first one

that enters your mind. You can always repeat this exercise with your other concerns, one at a time, as many times as necessary.

2. **Be practical!** Pick something that you're already yearning to overcome, something that's close to your heart.

3. **Start simple!** If this is the first time you're walking through these steps, you might want to save the more difficult issues for the next time around. Either way, walking your own path is courageous.

4. **Be relentless!** This is your path and nobody else's. The point of this exercise is only to guide you and to help you to stick to it.

Let's begin right where you are.

What's bothering you?

If you would give your experience a name, what would you call it?

The power of imagery is an amazing tool for helping us walk our own path. Many moments in life just come and go, but we do have the power to retain them. We can picture meaningful scenes in our minds and then later retrieve them. That allows us to relive those memories whenever it suits us best.

Many of our experiences have left us with lasting impressions. It's the negative events in our lives that tend to leave the most residue. Fortunately, these negative images are helpful in our efforts to demarcate the boundaries of the path that we are walking. A retelling of a negatively charged experience brings our story alive. We're the author of our story. And our personal narrative allows important themes to rise to the surface that are relevant for us today.

Take the time right now to think back and describe in detail what your experience was like when you last encountered your Antagonist.

I've included some guiding questions to help you develop your story below, but if they feel too cumbersome, set them aside and allow your story to unfold on its own.

YOUR ANTAGONIST STORY

- **I last experienced my Antagonist when I was...**
- **I was alone/together with...**

- Along with the emotional feelings, I also experienced: sweating / increased heart rate / tightness in chest / exhaustion / adrenaline rush / other...
- All I could think of doing was: running away / crawling into a hole / putting up a fight / fulfilling my need / other...
- What did I do? I did...
- Other relevant features of my story...

Here and Now

It's important to recall a negatively charged story because that's how we create a *benchmark* for ourselves. It's a reminder, a time when we encountered our Antagonist and things didn't really go to our liking. Maybe we gave in to our fear, our anxiety, or our addiction.

Maybe we felt ashamed or experienced regret. It could have been a very confusing, painful, and stressful time. Our Antagonist has the power to leave us feeling disoriented and even estranged from ourselves.

Being able to tap into this memory, to imagine ourselves telling our story in such detail, means that it's still with us. It's not just something that happened in the past. We're still carrying it around with us. Our ability to describe it in the *here and now* means that it's still alive.

That makes it a useful resource. It's not only the content of our story that matters, but also the context. You may see certain aspects of your story that are relevant to what's bothering you right now. If you didn't catch them, go back and ponder the themes that surfaced in your *Antagonist Story*, and decide which of them are relevant to your situation today.

Are there aspects of your story that appear to be relevant to your situation today? Please describe...

How long has this issue been bothering you?

BENEFIT THEORY

I have a theory. I call it the "Benefit Theory." If we've been carrying around an issue for a couple of weeks, a few months, or even years, we must be benefiting from it in some way. If we weren't benefiting from it, we would have dropped it a long time ago. It would no longer be a part of our consciousness or our vocabulary. People don't do something unless they see a benefit in doing it.

The Sages teach that a person doesn't overstep their boundaries unless they know they'll receive benefit from it.[1] If we're stuck in the muddy middle, and these particular thoughts and behaviors are still guiding our lives, I'd venture to say that we're not just dealing with a smidgen of benefit residue, but a great degree of it. It's just human nature. People don't do things that they don't benefit from.

When we become wiser to this and conscious of the fact that a particular thought or behavior is no longer working for us, we're able to develop a firm attitude toward our Antagonist. We henceforth won't be so quick to summon it to our door, let alone invite it in. If it arrives, we'll ignore it or simply tell it to get lost.

In line with Yehudah ben Teima, we leave it sitting on our porch, hinting to it that it no longer exists in our eyes. As long as it stays outside, it can't enter our line of vision. When we start to block its entrance into our circle of consciousness, that's when we know that we've placed ourselves back in the driver's seat.

Twist in Perspective

Our Antagonist hijacks our identity. Our behaviors then become representative of who we think we are. We've probably already given each one of them a name. We might say, "I'm a coffee drinker," "I'm a drug addict," "I'm a thrill seeker," or "I'm a downer."

But at the same time, people will complain, "I can't take it anymore; it's killing me." And I simply retort, "You need to convince me that you don't want it in your life anymore because it really looks like you're enjoying it. Nu! You're doing it all the time."

Does that sound too controversial? It's difficult to guide someone toward goodness if they're too busy benefiting from bad things.

I spoke at length with a person addicted to crack. He was working as a landscaper. Apparently, landscaping is good work for an addict. Every month, when he'd receive his paycheck, he'd cash it and spend

---

1. *Bava Metzia* 5b; *Shavuos* 42b; *Kiddushin* 62b.

the whole night smacked up on crack, and call in sick the next day. Somehow the job could afford him to miss a day or two. He was deeply in love with a woman who was the mother of their child, but she told him he wasn't invited to be a part of their lives. "It's because I'm such a mess," he said.

He came to therapy in order to sort out his relationship with this woman and their child. He claimed that living his life without them was his greatest struggle, but he had no desire to curb his crack habit.

Was he really making room for them in his life? He was too busy filling himself up with something else, and it was destructive to boot. One day a month of smoke appeared to be more valuable to him than they were. When I asked him if this had anything to do with his crack habit, he made it very clear that he wasn't willing to give up his one evening with the pipe.

So, too, with our harmful thoughts. When we find ourselves lost and confused, we may desire to rid ourselves of the negativity. But truth be told, like Jack and his relationship with anxiety, which we discussed in Chapter 7, we like to cling to it. We actually enjoy the emotional rush it has to offer.

You're a passionate person. You want to feel alive! However bad your behaviors are, you just can't help but want to hold on to those lively feelings. Our negative thoughts have the earthly ability to keep us charged. They tend to remind us that we're still alive and breathing. Although we may be actually drowning in them, they look as if they are our lifesaver.

YOUR BENEFIT STORY

I'd like you to take a moment to imagine how you may be benefiting from continuing this particular behavior or thought pattern. Think of an instance when you gave in to your Antagonist, but this time benefited from doing so.

- I spoke with a woman with severe anxiety who told me, "Before an exam, I really rely on those anxious sensations. The butterflies in my stomach actually give me the energy to focus on my thoughts. I always know I'll do much better on a test when my stomach is all a mess."

- A fellow who indicated that his marriage was crumbling as a result of his lifetime ritual of self-isolation, proudly said, "I've accomplished so much in my work. I'm well-published, and I've become a leader in my field because I isolate myself."

It's a real *twist in perspective* when we realize that it's possible that we've been holding on to our greatest concerns—i.e., our anxieties, fears, shame, guilt, desires, and doubts—because we might miss them, along with the benefits that they provide.

I've included the following guiding questions below to help you elucidate your *Benefit Story*. Please describe a time when you gave in to your Antagonist and how you benefited from doing so.

- **Once I experienced my Antagonist when I was…**
- **I was alone/together with…**
- **All I could think about was…**
- **I benefited from giving into my Antagonist by…**
- **Now that I know that I'm benefiting from this behavior or thought pattern, am I actually willing to stop experiencing it completely? Yes/No**
- **If your answer is no, stop here (you've completed the exercise). The positive benefits that you receive from maintaining your current relationship with your Antagonist appear to outweigh the negatives. You're choosing to continue suffering from the negative consequences in order to receive those positive benefits.**
- **If your answer is yes, you're ready to continue on to Chapter 23 and start building a Peace Treaty with your Antagonist.**

TAKEAWAYS

- We can picture meaningful scenes in our mind and then later retrieve them, allowing us to relive those memories whenever it suits us best.

- Describing our negative story in the here and now allows us to identify important themes that are relevant for us today.
- If we've been carrying around this issue for weeks, months, or even years, we must be benefiting from it in some way.
- Once we're conscious of the fact that this particular thought or behavior is no longer working for us, we're able to develop a firm attitude toward our Antagonist.
- It's a real twist in perspective when you realize that it's possible that you've been holding on to your greatest concerns because you might miss them, along with the benefits that they provide.

Chapter 23

Peace Treaty

W e may be at war with our Antagonist, but in line with the Slonimer Rebbe, it doesn't behoove us to attack it head-on. In order to remove ourselves from its bad ways, we must first seek the good. The only way to serve everyone's best interests in a heated relationship is to pursue peace. Our ability to separate the good from the bad is by definition the first act toward establishing *shalom*. The next step is a wise one: to purposely create a *ceasefire* that will allow us to establish *shalom* with our Antagonist in consonance with our own terms.

CEASEFIRE

The moment that we give our Antagonist a name, we're free to create an emotional disconnect. We do this by recognizing it for what it truly is—an entity in and of itself. This is the first step toward establishing a *peace treaty* with it.

Shalom grants us the space and freedom to see through its cunning schemes and exposes the deceptive role that our Antagonist has been playing in our life's story. Until now, it's been cleverly drawing us in, bombarding us with its misleading messages. It's been directing us off track. Its rhetoric has been convincing, and we've felt compelled to take its advice.

But we no longer have to be tricked into thinking that it's acting in our best interests. We don't have to continue walking down the path upon which it has been leading us. We can decide not to listen or give in. We don't have to continue living according to its script. We may author our own story and stipulate the role that we want our Antagonist to play in our lives for the future.

We no longer have to let it define who we are.

Celebrate the fact that what's been gnawing at you isn't who you really are. It's simply a useful tool to help you move forward as you walk your own path.

We've been steadily working to arrive at this point. You've identified your Antagonist, labeled it, and started to distance yourself from it. You've taken the initial step necessary to establish *shalom* with it. Seize this moment to create a peace treaty with your greatest adversary on your own terms.

It's time to establish a ceasefire that will briefly end the conflict. Freedom builds character. Draft an agreement that will respect your need for self-determination. When you're finished, you'll be able to boldly say, "You're you, and I'm me. I have no influence over you, and you no longer have any influence over me."

YOUR PEACE TREATY

Shalom may only exist between two distinct and separate entities. It's maintained by adhering to strict borders. Have the following four steps in mind as you begin writing your peace treaty:

1. Create an image of your Antagonist in your mind. It can be in the form of a person, an energy, or even an object.
2. Ponder your differences and appreciate its distinctiveness.
3. Initiate an open conversation with it and arrive at a mutual understanding, one that respects your need for self-determination.
4. While composing your narrative, make sure to describe in full detail your separate roles and responsibilities. Focus on your values. Keep in mind that you're the author of your story. That means you have the last word. So don't hesitate to write down all of your demands!

Imagine yourself speaking directly to your Antagonist. What would you care to say to it? Below are some thoughtful guidelines. Feel free to use your own language when initiating and describing the conversation. It's important to jot everything down. Nothing brings us more clarity than being able to read through our own words, again and again. There's healing power in the back and forth, in the give and take.

- **I want to end the conflict because...**
- **My demands are...**
- **Our separate roles are...**
- **I'm determined to keep the peace because...**

Maybe it would be helpful to take a look at how some other people managed to create *shalom*, enact a ceasefire, and draw up a peace treaty with their own Antagonist.

LEAH'S HERMIT

Most people enjoy the occasional company of others, but I met a young woman who made it clear from the onset that she was the exception to the rule. Leah is a self-proclaimed hermit. She smiled, saying, "Non-social behavior is my norm. Being in a big house all by myself is great. Nobody bothers me." She revealed that people tend to rub her the wrong way, stating, "Many people just upset me, so it's my inclination to stay away."

Although this has been Leah's modus operandi, she has started to recognize the downside to living the hermit life. "It's my nature to be alone, but I've started to notice that the less time I spend with people, the less comfortable I end up being around them. It doesn't make me want to be around people anymore," she reflected.

Being in this difficult situation at home gave Leah plenty of food for thought. She was becoming wiser to the negative influence that her non-social behavior was having on her. She said, "This may be how I normally feel, but I know intellectually that it's not healthy to spend this much time alone."

Being mindful of the perils of hermithood inspired her to make a shift. She reported, "I'm trying to get out more. I'm trying to put myself in a position where I'm around people more. I'm really making an effort. It's like you say, it's about being proactive. I started reaching out to people. I've been using WhatsApp and sending out emails, asking if they'd be interested in hosting me for Shabbos. Shabbos stinks when I'm alone."

She paused and pondered out loud, "When I go to visit friends, I do look forward to it. I'm even happy when I'm there. But I normally don't want to do it. I don't want to leave the house." In spite of her Antagonist's house arrest, she was clever enough to figure out a way to escape from its sticky hold. She happily reported, "I've been purposely reaching out to the people I'm closest to. I only message the friends and families who I like. I now have Shabbos booked for the next two months."

Leah knows more about who plays a positive role in her life. Knowing what's good for her has allowed her to feel more in charge. She's more apt to do for herself what she imagines to be in her best interests. In order to continue gaining the upper hand, I suggested that her next step forward should be to create a peace treaty with her Antagonist. She nodded her head in agreement.

I began by asking, "Why, exactly, would you like to end the conflict with your hermit?"

Leah answered, "Because, intellectually speaking, I know that it will be better for me emotionally in the long run. In the short run, it might also be better for me. Evidence to this is that my feelings of loneliness have dissipated just by reaching out to these other people."

As we discussed the importance of establishing a ceasefire, she stated thoughtfully, "Being the hermit is the portion of being alone that is uncomfortable for me—but being non-social isn't always a negative."

I questioned, "Are you saying that the benefits of being a hermit outweigh its downside? Are you sure that you really want to put an end to the conflict? Maybe it's more important that you have your alone time."

"There's a part of being alone that isn't negative. I need to be alone for at least some portion of every day. I can't have people persistently being around me. But once I've gone past my fill, no, it's not pleasant. The reason I would like to end the conflict with the hermit is because of this very unpleasant feeling," she concluded.

Using her power of distinction, Leah managed to differentiate between her positive need for being alone versus the negativity she experiences while being a hermit. What an important distinction! I was curious what tools she was planning to implement the next time the hermit decided to take charge and regain control of their relationship.

Leah had some suggestions. "The first thing I'll do is leave my house. Maybe I'll go to the market and buy some fruit, or like today, go on a run around the neighborhood. I might even just sit in the park and schmooze with some of the ladies. When I sense that I'm slipping into this non-social behavior, it'd be good to try and connect to someone else."

While continuing to establish a peace treaty with her negative behavior, I announced, "From here on in, you get to decide the rules and parameters of your relationship with the hermit."

Leah showed assertiveness. "It's my longer-term attempt to put the hermit in its place. If it bothers me, I'll say to it, 'I don't need any of your hermit-ism right now. And if you don't abide by my rules, I'm just gonna leave. I'll just walk out of the house. I'll leave you all alone, all to yourself.' That's exactly what happened today. I left and went running on a new trail."

I asked Leah if she was determined to keep the peace between herself and the hermit. Her response was, "Absolutely! And I'll tell you why. I went out one evening last week with two friends and saw myself in a new light. I noticed that I had gained access to a particular aspect of myself, a part of my identity, that I don't normally have access to. I thought to myself, *I'm one of the girls. And I have access to this now—it's natural.* I don't seem to have access to this when I'm not around them."

Not only did Leah not feel lonely that evening, but it also gave her the opportunity to help a friend in need. "My friend was going through a depressing time, and while speaking to her, a unique and familiar expression of myself surfaced. It's a different me. One that doesn't normally have the opportunity to come out. It was quite magical. My friend even expressed how magical it was, saying, 'It's really great hearing you talk so freely.' I was telling her helpful stories. I was reaching out to her and speaking directly to her situation. I understand depression and pain, so much so that people don't have to feel that way when they're around me."

As our conversation came to an end, Leah stated resolutely, "I'm not going to allow this negative non-social behavior to take control anymore. And that's because of the opportunities that surface when I'm not around it. I like being able to connect to these different parts of my personality. I'm allowed to fully shine. It's much nicer than the discomfort that the hermit provides."

ZACK'S ANIMOSITY

Zack preferred not to eat the food that was served in his yeshiva. He liked to cook food that was healthier. And if someone wanted to join in and help him prepare the food, he was happy for them to get involved. Sharing brought him much joy.

This was all fine and dandy until he stumbled into a conversation that managed to sour his view. He seemed bothered as he shared the story, pointing out, "I used to always give people food, but one day, a person came up to me and said, 'Why do you give away everything you have?' This is something that even my family has said to me in the past."

This message managed to arouse Zack's Antagonist. Once it stepped in, things really snowballed. He revealed, "I didn't really feel that way, but then I heard that external voice. And then on top of that, another person in the yeshiva started rebuking the other guys, saying, 'Why are you taking this guy's food?' And then all of a sudden, I started thinking that way, too. I thought, *Yeah, why are these people taking all my food?*"

Knowing that his Antagonist's view had taken hold, he paused a moment to mourn the loss of this particular aspect of himself. He shared in wonder, "Until that point, I didn't even think about it. I just enjoyed sharing my food with other people. And then someone came along and said these things and I started feeling this animosity toward other people. It happened so quickly. I had lost the feeling of togetherness that I once had. The next thing I knew, I didn't enjoy giving away my food anymore. It was weird."

Stressing how foreign of an idea this was for him, Zack clarified, "The anger and animosity I was having was a new thing. It wasn't in me before; it didn't even feel natural. In order to express my new dislike of people's behavior, I had to arouse the anger for it to work. Otherwise, it wouldn't." In order to fulfill his Antagonist's script, Zack had to go against his normal giving nature. "I once had an innocence. I thought it was just normal to share one's food with other people," he lamented.

While telling over his negatively charged story, Zack soon became conscious of how he implements the same old approach in his life today. "Wow! I find myself needing to arouse this animosity in myself when people ask favors from me. For example, in my repair business, people are always asking me to fix this or that, saying, 'Can you just take care of this little thing for me?' This is my profession, and they're taking advantage of me. They don't realize it, but it's like they're stealing from me," he said with concern.

Thinking back to his time in yeshiva, he was in awe of the scope of influence that his Antagonist had. It had really done a number on him at the time. He articulated, "It got so bad that I had gotten to the point where I even started looking at the staff in a negative way. I started to look at the whole yeshiva as the problem."

Zack indicated that his attitude about the yeshiva shifted a few years ago. He had a change of heart, stating, "I started to think, what is this inside of me? What am I thinking?" He looked at me and said, "If you knew what was going on inside my head, it would be terrible, but for some reason I persisted with it. How could the entire yeshiva be so bad? It sounded so wrong that I decided to take a step aside and, bit by bit, I was able to remove myself from these thoughts."

He added with a smile, "Like you say, I wasn't benefiting from it anymore. It was just hurting me. And I'd think, *Oh my gosh. Why do I have to think this way?* The only way I could make peace with it was by saying, 'It's not good for me. I'm just going to chill out about it.'"

Realizing that his animosity was no longer serving his best interests, I suggested that he take the next step and create a peace treaty with his Antagonist.

"Why do you want to end the conflict?" I began.

He said resolutely, "I want to end the battle with the animosity because it doesn't bring good to anyone. To the victim or the perpetrator. I want to end it because I realize that it's not an important thing to have in my life. It's even taught me that most battles aren't really worthwhile. Most battles like this are not worth fighting."

Now that he thought more about it, Zack added, "It's never served me well. This intolerance is a form of self-servitude. It's haughty. It's like having a battle with another person. It's not worth it. It's just going to take you down with it. It takes away my own happiness."

"If you could speak to it directly, what would you say to the animosity?" I asked. Zack sat up in his seat and voiced, "'Hey, animosity, get away from me. You take away all my happiness and all the things I value."

He had already created *shalom* with his Antagonist, called a ceasefire, and had begun drafting a peace treaty. Zack sounded sincere, but I still needed a little bit of convincing. He shared earlier that when people ask favors from him—making him feel uncomfortable and slighted—animosity is the very tool he uses to protect himself, meaning that animosity, however negative, plays a role in his life today. So, I suggested, "Maybe it's just enough to learn how to manage animosity. As you establish your peace treaty, have in mind whether there's any benefit to keeping the animosity around. You get to stipulate if, when, and where it is deemed acceptable in your life."

"Honestly," said Zack, "I don't think animosity has anything to offer me. Instead of using animosity as the thing to keep me away from bad things, I feel like there's got to be a different way. There's got to be another way to keep me safe from those potential issues."

"That sounds great!" I said. "We'll eventually get to that step." I then inquired, "So, in your new relationship with your animosity, what boundaries are you planning to set?"

Zack looked introspectively at the animosity in his heart and declared, "I'm not gonna need your services anymore. I'm more interested in finding a new way to deal with these situations."

"Okay, now that you're back in charge, what are your separate roles going to be?" I asked.

Gazing back at animosity, he said, "You can be animosity all on your own as long as I have no part in it. Your services have not helped me." He paused. "Hmm, but there are some truly bad things in life, so maybe there is something you can offer me. Maybe there's a way of utilizing your services without you becoming me."

Zack's animosity continues to have an alluring effect on him. Yet, he sounded earnest, so I recommended saying, "When I find an area of life in which I could use your services, I'll be in touch with you." Or similarly, "At some point in the future your services might be needed. Don't call me, I'll call you."

He appeared to want to maintain the *shalom*, so at the end of the meeting, I asked, "Why are you so determined to keep the peace?"

"I'm determined to keep this *shalom* for a couple reasons. First, I don't see animosity as serving my best interests. Second, the less animosity I have, the more I recognize that there's no drawback to *not* having it around," Zack concluded.

TAKEAWAYS

- The moment you can give your Antagonist a name, you'll be able to create an emotional disconnect by recognizing it for what it truly is—an entity in and of itself.
- *Shalom* grants you the space and freedom to see through its cunning schemes and exposes the deceptive role that your Antagonist has been playing in your story.
- You can author your own story and control whatever role your Antagonist is going to play in your personal narrative for the future.
- Establishing a ceasefire will end the conflict, and drafting an agreement that respects your need for self-determination removes the influence it currently has on you.

Chapter 24

Building Confidence

Y ou've created a peace treaty with your Antagonist, and you're no longer required to define yourself by the expectations and external messages that it has to offer. Now that you're free from its influence, you may freely rewrite your story and walk the path that you see before you.

THE ROAD TO CONFIDENCE

One of the secrets to walking our own path is to be conscious of the fact that we've always been on our own path and that we continue to be on our own path. When feeling down, anxious, or out of control, we may perceive ourselves as being off track, but in truth, we haven't veered away from our path at all.

As we've clarified, our Antagonist clouds our mind, filling it with damaging thoughts and ideas. It manipulates us into feeling less grounded, leaving us with a faulty view of our path as being distant and hidden. But at this point, we've become wiser to our Antagonist's antics. We've started to see through the illusion. We see our path before us, and we're putting our best foot forward.

In line with King David, this doesn't mean that we're not going to stumble. Just be aware that there are people who, when they stumble, end up feeling unsure and thus wallow in their mistakes. We can be our own worst enemies. And then the Antagonist unleashes its message: "You slipped up again. You'll never get it right. Why bother trying anymore?"

Walking with confidence is what keeps us on track. It's an attitude, and it's a value. Every opportunity to pull oneself out of the muddy middle is a confidence builder. And as we continue to live according to what we truly value, it will require a much thicker wall of deception to deter us.

Whether we feel sorry for ourselves or not, just like King David, we must ask ourselves this essential question: "Okay. Here I am again. I'm stuck in this uncomfortable situation again, but now what? Where do I go from here?"

We've started to get a handle on our overflow. As we know, what we fill ourselves up with determines our path. It consumes our thoughts, and it directly affects our behavior. We get to choose with what to fill ourselves. When we're feeling stuck, it's upon us to take pause to reflect, refill, and redirect.

Our path is back in our own hands; we've become more self-assured in our life, in our work, and in our relationships. With eyes forward, we're maintaining trajectory. We're staying practical, being positive, and keeping what we value at the forefront.

HEADING OUT

As we continue to stride forward, we tend to encounter many new beginnings. Like with any journey, before we head out, it's best to first pack our bags. But it's impossible to bring everything we want if we're being weighed down by unnecessary baggage.

Take a moment right now to imagine yourself unpacking the extra weight and consciously leaving behind the external messages and behaviors that have been misleading you. Messages like "You're incapable," or, "This will never work," only get in the way. They slow you down. And if you don't manage to discard them all, it's OK. Most people aren't able to unload their bags completely. It's not always clear what to leave behind.

The key to confidently navigating your own path is knowing what essentials to take along with you on your journey. Filling your bags with what you consider to be most meaningful is the path to putting your best foot forward.

Take a moment to ask yourself what it is that you want to bring along with you.

Filling our bags with what we value makes the journey worthwhile. Use this moment to pack your bags with the essentials of life. Such items may include connection, individuality, security, and messages like "I have purpose," and "What I value actually matters."

Make sure to bring a load of confidence! It's again time to stride forward. Take your next step by making a list of the values and positive messages that you treasure in life. Feel free to write them down. As we've said, it's your story—you get to decide how to tell it.

TAKEAWAYS

- When feeling down, anxious, or out of control, you may perceive yourself as being off track, but in truth, you haven't veered away from your path at all.
- Every opportunity to pull yourself out of the muck is a confidence builder.
- Before you head out, make sure to pack your bags with what you truly value.
- Tell your story in your own way.

Finale

ALL THE WISER

Y ou've become wiser to your Antagonist's whims and freed yourself from its influence. You've successfully established a peace treaty that better suits your interests and tweaked your story to work to your own benefit. Please take a moment to rest easy, for you are finally standing on solid ground.

You've earned it.

You're finally in touch with your *whereabouts*.

You're no longer willing to deny yourself the pleasure of living according to who you truly are, and what you truly value. And I can't stress this enough: As a *tzelem Elokim*, a being formed in Hashem's image, this means that you're actually standing on your own two feet. You've taken great strides in a short time—your mind is clear and you see the path before you.

But take it from me, before you decide to gaze upon what may lie ahead, it behooves you (and me) to take this moment to breathe.

None of us lack challenges. They gain our attention and warrant our time and effort, yet they need to be governed. And in truth, that's exactly what our Antagonist is truly hoping for. It wants us to control it and to guide it, and it yearns to find its completion in us.

And now we're all the wiser for it. We've figured out a few things. We know that when we commit ourselves to taking a step forward, our next job is to zone in on the task at hand. We learned that the follow-through doesn't just refine us, it also defines us. And we can always take solace in the fact that if we end up stumbling again—deep into the muddy middle—our issue is only a technical one.

That means that there's always a solution to our problems.

The next time you find yourself overtaken by fear, shame, anxiousness, or confusion, it shouldn't take too long to identify your exact location. You'll know, unequivocally, that you're stuck amid the same old muddy mess. And you'll remember that your only recourse is to get your legs moving.

You'll make a run for it.

And when you're once again standing on solid ground, you may be certain that your next step will be pointed in the right direction. This is a golden opportunity. You're invited to become the best version of yourself that you can be!

We're all yearning for this. There's nothing more rewarding than stepping into the shoes of the person we've been seeking to be. This is a big deal. We all deserve a taste of what it means to be authentically ourselves.

We're hungry for it. And that's a good thing. Since there are many facets to our personalities, we'll never be lacking anything on our plate. There will always be something that demands our attention.

Although you're all the wiser, I'll take a shot in the dark and assume that there are a few other things about yourself that may be bothering you right now. If so, you're invited to go back and walk any one of your immediate concerns through the exercise above.

Remember to keep it relevant. Be the simpleton! Sweat only the small stuff.

If you have any technical questions along the way, I suggest that you go back and reexamine the concepts, tools, and guiding principles in this book. And for your benefit, you're also welcome to take a gander at the Key Points that I've outlined below.

It's essential to take time to celebrate your achievements. You've made it out of the muddy middle! The next time you find yourself stuck in the muck, you may remember the solid ground on which you are currently standing. And know that when life gets sticky, you can always let your legs do the walking.

When we feel lost and far from home, we can always turn ourselves right around. We feel most free from our Antagonist when we are homeward bound.

Appendix: Key Points

Chapter 1: Your Antagonist

- You're the major character in your story.
- Your Antagonist is an opposing force.
- It wants to see you struggle.
- It distorts your vision.
- It blurs the lenses of how you view yourself and the world around you.
- It's deceptive.
- You have your struggles like everyone else.
- You're already wiser in some ways, and less wise in others.
- The Antagonist wants you to do the wrong thing.
- Identifying with its messages leads to feelings of emptiness, distress, and tension.

Chapter 2: It's a Bother

- You've probably already given what's bothering you a name.
- A diagnostician breaks down behaviors and patterns into simple terms.
- You've placed labels upon yourself.

- Basing your life's decisions on these labels sends you right into the muddy middle.
- When you're free of labels, you're free to walk your own path.
- Your own values should be the basis of your life's decisions.
- You may change your relationship with your Antagonist and write your own story.
- Understand your Antagonist's ways, or it will continue to rule over you.

SECTION II: CLEVER OR WISE

Chapter 3: The Wise Person: Yehudah ben Teima

The Eagle

- Eagles see from above with a bird's-eye view.
- You may avert your eyes from negativity.
- Looking at the wrong thing causes you to lose sight of yourself.
- You may zero in on what suits you best.
- A bird's-eye view gives you perspective and helps you to maintain trajectory along your path.
- Eyes are impressionable. External influences, like foreign messages and expectations, slip through your lenses, so you must close them every day to negative messages.
- The eagle eye is proactive, not reactive.

The Lion

- Walking your path demands perseverance.
- The heart is home to inspiration and choice: you choose whether to walk down a good path or a bad one.
- You're the king of the jungle!
- Yehudah ben Teima believes that you may catch yourself en route, question any rush of desire, and take charge.
- Making mistakes makes you wiser to the ways of your desires.

The Deer

- Legs are made for action and are built to do goodness.

- Legs invite goodness into your life and into the lives of others, and they get you in and out of sticky situations.
- Focusing on what you truly value is always an invitation to approach life from the inside-out.
- A change of scenery may make you feel more secure.

The Leopard

- Although brazenness should normally be avoided, you can be shameless in the face of negative outside forces.
- A wise person has a strong constitution and holds a positive self-regard.
- The Antagonist distracts you from doing the right thing.
- It speaks to you in your own language.
- A leopard is solitary and wears blinders.
- In order to avoid getting in the muck, you must remain unabashed in the face of adversity.

Chapter 4: The Clever Person: King David

- Reverses Yehudah ben Teima's order of things.
- The path toward becoming a wise person is a clever one.
- Only the wise may protect/redirect their eyes from eye candy.
- King David is an archetype of someone who is always finding themselves in a sticky situation.
- He has a clever method to free oneself of unhealthy desires, negative external influences, and self-evading pursuits.

Your Only Recourse

- When your thinking has already been corrupted, your only recourse is to get your legs moving.
- Change your location, change your perspective.
- The key to becoming more cunning is to first be in touch with your whereabouts.
- Self-awareness is what allows you to take pause to reflect and redirect.
- Feel lost? Imagine the last place you stumbled. You're still there.

- Moving your legs activates your heart and enables your eyes to see clearly.
- Like you, King David is always finding himself in the muddy middle.
- Maybe it's time to speak to a spiritual doctor.

SECTION III: THE SCHMUTZ

Chapter 5: Corrective Lenses

- When your lenses are caked over, your perception becomes corrupted.
- You're made from Hashem's first thought—His Torah.
- When all seems lost, it's not really gone—it's only been covered up.

Layers of Schmutz

- The lenses you sport directly affect how you define yourself and engage with the world around you.
- If you've been focused on externalities, your view of the world has most likely become compromised.
- It's better to look within.

It's Totally Crazy

- You have to have crazy thoughts to do anything wrong.
- Deficiency is at the heart of wrongdoing.
- What you see is what you get.
- In murky waters, people compensate by reaching for externals.

Crippling Quagmire

- Walking someone else's path and not your own is likened to living a life captured in a murky prison.
- The Antagonist covers your eyes with clay to create a partition or barrier between you and the world.
- It fools you into following a different path.

- In the darkest of places, King David looks to Hashem to drag him out.
- It's easy to be whisked away by external forces.
- It's not worth fighting your Antagonist head on.
- Only with Hashem's aid are you able to return to a clean bill of health. Call to Hashem!
- You're either moving forward or backward.

World Corruption

- Misdeeds and physical desire strain your eyes.
- Don't ask to be tested.

A Bad Eye

- A bad eye propels you into exile.
- Jealousy is a prison.
- Eying what your friends have with a crooked lens brings ill upon you and your friends.
- Jealousy blinds you with a heavy darkness and engenders a hatred of others.
- When you're unhappy with your lot, you don't even receive what you were allotted.
- Trying to possess that which is outside of our own domain is humanity's downfall.
- Gazing upon another's possessions leaves you conflicted.

Blind Spots

- The more schmutz that gets in the way, the more numerous our spots become over time.
- Our view gets distorted: what is negative looks positive, and what looks negative is actually positive.

Chapter 6: The Eagle Eye

A Wise Lens

- Wise people avert their eyes and focus on their best interests.

Between Friends

- When your lenses are caked with schmutz, it messes with the perception you have of yourself and the world around you.
- In murky waters, people compensate by reaching for unhealthy externals. Trying to possess that which is outside of their own domain means they are unhappy with their lot.
- You're always on the go, moving either forward or backward.
- The more schmutz that gets in a person's way, the more numerous their blind spots grow over time, and the more distorted their view becomes (what's negative looks positive, and what looks negative is actually positive).
- When Hashem wakes you up in the morning and wipes the soot from your eyes, your field of perception is no longer encumbered with the schmutz, granting you a fresh start and a new perspective.

SECTION IV: YOUR WHEREABOUTS

Chapter 7: Power of Distinction

- Off balance? It's because you've lost sight of your own limits.
- It's important to differentiate the line between who you are and the world around you.

Being Myself

- It's difficult to harness your power of distinction while caught feeling sidelined.
- The tension, stress, and discomfort that comes along with this is a call to action!
- You may always locate yourself somewhere along your very own Being Myself spectrum.
- There's a particular aspect of yourself that doesn't like being yourself.

Life Preserver

- It's nearly impossible to locate your whereabouts when stuck in preservation mode.
- Your struggle often becomes both your foe and your life preserver.

Power of Preservation

- Denying any part of yourself forms a gap between the different aspects of yourself, depriving you of the ability to differentiate and catapulting you into a state of personal discord.
- When you reintegrate yourself with the rest of yourself, your anxiety dissipates.
- The moment you feel distressed and become anxious, your power of preservation quickly swoops to the rescue.
- Preservation is a coping mechanism that may be applied to future events. You just have to guide it!

Been There, Done That

- Experience builds attitude.
- It's important to recognize your concern as having its own power.
- It's your power of distinction that permits you to see your Antagonist for what it really is, and to see yourself as a whole being and independent entity.
- Setting yourself apart is what transforms you into a real mensch.

Chapter 8: Persona Non Grata

Outside-In

- Introjection: Adopting worldly views and moving "the boundary of the world so far inside ourselves that there is almost nothing left of us."
- You're a nobody without a world of your own.

Inside-Out

- Decisions and choices must start from within the inner chambers of your heart.
- Working from the inside-out inspires your heart to guide your eyes in a more favorable direction.
- This means letting the right messages filter in, focusing on the best in people, and illustrating in your mind the necessary positive images that help you to reach your life's goals.
- An outside-in approach is superficial.
- Fighting directly against one's negative force is reactive, not proactive.

Inside-In

- Assume that you can't move anyone further than you've moved yourself.
- A delivery system from the inside to the inside, a heart-to-heart.
- Personal transformation is a private matter.

Chapter 9: Patterns

- There are people who appear to keep on keeping on, but for them, moving on really means that they're falling back into their old routine.

Foreseeable Patterns

- One action may be enough to inspire a person to repeat it.
- The reward for one negative action is another negative act.
- Choosing what's in your best interest is choosing life!
- Any slipup forms a gap between you and Hashem, and this opens you up to the negative influence of the outside world.
- Inertia: stuck in a negative flow.
- Tripping up is one thing, but enjoying it is another.

Power of Return

- Deciding not to repeat your action in the same scenario returns you back to your initial state. You're still kosher!

- A wise person knows that one overstep doesn't have to mean that you're bound to relive it.
- You can crack any habit by mobilizing your power of return. It's just easier when negativity hasn't yet taken hold.

Habituation

- It takes two to three tries under the same condition for an action to take full hold.
- When you've begun to define yourself by it—meaning that for whatever reason you've started to own it—you've fully dedicated yourself to it.

Themes

- Negative actions become the ruling theme when you repeat them. It's frustrating when you can't seem to move on.
- Returning to a person's norm may just be a part of an unhealthy cycle. This recycled theme is called organized chaos.

Your Norm

- There's safety in routine, so why change?
- Actualizing negative thoughts makes them appear to be a part of who you are. It gives your life purpose.
- These negative thoughts become your point of reference and basis for life's decisions, and the lens through which you view your world and the world around you.

The Third Link

- Because unhealthy behavior is a direct result of first actions, it makes it seem that there's no end to it. We are doomed to repeat it!
- However, there's a break. The second link is surely linked to the first, and the third is obviously connected to the second, but it's *nivdal*—disassociated from the very first.
- The third link is your ticket out. You don't have to be stuck feeling like just another link in the chain.

- The gap between the first and third link turns the third action into a brand-new thing, a new animal. Any desire to continue your behavior is going to be solely based on a new and different reason. It serves a new function.
- The third link allows you to do the wise thing and to question, "Is continuing this action really in my best interests? Is it who I am?"
- You don't have to be ruled by inertia. You can always stop to inquire, "Is it worth continuing with this particular behavior or thought pattern?"
- Unleash your power of imagery and imagine yourself boldly snipping away at the chain with a pair of ethereal metal clippers.

SECTION V: THE DAILY GR IND

Chapter 10: The Hungry Bear

The Beast Within

- There's a bear-like beast that lives within all of us. It seeks to consume. It will not rest until it can swallow up everything in the universe.

Inner Hunger

- Inner hunger causes a person to go out on the prowl. When we crave, the hungry bear takes hold, and our only concern is to fill the empty hole.
- "Hunger isn't life itself," says Rabbi Dessler. It's just there to keep us alive.
- Your heart's intentions can either be for the good or for the bad.
- Once feeling hungry, you won't just be hungry for now. You'll also hunger for the future.
- The more you attempt to indulge your cravings, the more intense your hunger will be.

Your Lot

- ‣ Latching on to externals just means that you're trying to extend your territory, your personal domain.
- ‣ All efforts to explore outside of yourself are in vain.
- ‣ You will find answers to your hungry energy by looking within.
- ‣ Your heart yearns to reach beyond itself. It's your natural inclination to want to do the right thing for yourself and for the people around you.

Need for Attachment

- ‣ Your hunger is spiritual in nature.
- ‣ It inspires you to want to connect to something which is much greater than yourself.
- ‣ You yearn to cling to the infinite.
- ‣ Doing acts of kindness for others satisfies your need for attachment.
- ‣ Your Antagonist sugarcoats everything.

The Honeytrap

- ‣ Running after what your heart and eyes desire leads you astray.
- ‣ What your heart seeks, you shall find. It's a self-fulfilling prophecy!
- ‣ Moshe tells us that once caught in the honeytrap, you feel satiated—but only for a fleeting moment.
- ‣ The Antagonist may exploit your strongest appetites, but it's really just a bunch of empty calories.

Chapter 11: Eye Candy

- • When you're hyper-focused on your eyes, you can then in turn guard your heart, preventing you from dancing right into the store.

- Moshe counseled us not to explore outside of ourselves because he knew that looking toward externals would cause us to go astray.
- Wise people are able to avert their eyes and not to seek that which they desire.
- When something catches your eye, it's your heart that tells you, "You've gotta have it."

Insatiable

- It's easy to judge yourself too harshly when you've given in to your cravings.
- People are known to wallow in their mistakes. It's a clever way to permit oneself to continue feeling down.
- You become so used to it that you can even forget why you started to relish it in the first place.

Complacency

- Laziness leads to complacency.
- When in a low place, your efforts to climb out are often met with opposition.

A Brand-New Routine

- A bad routine takes off the edge, but the relief is only short-lived.
- It's hard to change routine.
- You may leave those old routines behind by doing something good for yourself or a friend.
- Hashem will help you see it to completion.
- Satiate your appetites with the good!
- Doing acts of kindness curbs your appetites, and in time, you'll have transformed yourself into becoming a real mensch.

Chapter 12: Mighty as a Lion

Roaring Outa Bed

- Every morning, Hashem provides you with new clarity and gives your heart the courage to tackle your newly updated world.

- Thank Hashem for kindly rebooting your soul!
- Gratitude is what speaks to the wisdom in your heart, awakens a spiritual hunger, and permits you to serve Hashem with all your might.
- "A person should be mighty like a lion to stand up in the morning to serve his creator" (Rav Yosef Caro).

Commitment

- "Knowing is only half the battle" (G.I. Joe).
- The heart is the pivotal place from which you commit to either go down a good path or a bad one.
- Life is about choices.
- Making the right choice is what activates and actualizes the wisdom in your heart.
- In order to truly seize the day, you must take the lead.

King of the Beasts

- The morning is the most opportune time to take command of the day.
- Hashem crowned you as the King of the Beasts!
- With the right get-up-and-go, a leader's day is bound to be filled with positive energy.
- Leaving your heart to its own tricks isn't the wise way to go. It leads to making mistakes.
- The more you add to the shmutz, the more it takes away from your efforts to pursue your goals for the day.
- Your Antagonist tries to take advantage by encouraging inauthentic thoughts to arise from the vacuous space in your heart, seize your mind, and corrupt your vision.
- Engaging with your internal wisdom sets you free and provides you with a proper shift in perspective.
- First mourn for the initial misemployment of the wisdom in your heart, and then speak to your heart, telling it to cry out to Hashem.

Power of Choice

- Hashem watches you closely, and yet at the same time allows you to choose your own destiny.
- Your ability to choose between good and bad grants you the means to forge and maintain your own path.
- The power is in your hands to choose to become either lofty or lowly.
- Choose life!
- It's upon you to make good on the good, or as Rabbi Tucazinsky puts it, it's upon you to "make your own good."

Chapter 13: Decisions

- The moment you make a decision, you'll be struck with FOMO and be filled with regret.
- It's your Antagonist that makes you think that making a decision automatically excludes all the other options.

Loss of Possibility

- Any choice you make cuts you immediately off from any other possibility.
- One decision and you're already mourning the loss of possibility.

Black or White

- An outside-in approach is simpler because you may at least define yourself by what you think you're not.
- An inside-out approach requires that you already know what you're packing: your personal strengths and what you truly value.
- It doesn't pay to be bashful when making educated decisions in life.
- Life is often fuzzy and gray, but decisions must be an "all-or-nothing"!
- Making a commitment means taking a stance. Putting up boundaries is a bold move.

- The regret that seeps in after making a decision only muddies your thoughts, and you start to question who you are and how you define yourself.
- Limits put up walls, but they also open doorways. A black-or-white decision unlocks the gateways to your greatest potential.

Educated Decisions

- Do your own research, get professional advice, and listen to others share their own experiences.
- Allow yourself a trial period when starting something new. Make sure it's also black or white!
- You may always reevaluate things once you've reached your mark.
- Educated decisions set up healthy boundaries. They're like guardrails that help you maintain trajectory while walking down your own path.

Blinders

- Good decisions demand that you wear blinders.
- The sharper your choices, the clearer your path will be.
- Not sticking to your commitments means that you haven't truly committed yourself to carrying out the task.

Stick to It

- The three components of a wise person's success in this world: persistence, consistency, and visualization of follow-through.
- Every time you stumble and pick yourself up, you build confidence.

Chapter 14: Bold as a Leopard

Stiff-Necked

- The way to handle a stiff-necked personality is to match its toughness and also be as hard as metal.

Too Bashful

- A non-brazen person will naturally seek relaxation, and timid people tend to be more complacent.
- Humble, modest, or timid people are too complacent.
- Brazen people are on fire! They don't settle.

Stouthearted

- The mighty, powerful, and leopard-like personality can be used for the good or for the bad. You can motivate it either to go against your grain, or to hold yourself tight to your path.
- Yehudah ben Teima indicates that being unabashed in the face of the Antagonist's opposition allows you to avoid it altogether.
- Arouse your wise cardiac output by speaking to your heart! This sets up a proper roadblock, guarding you from stepping away from the path that stretches out before you.
- Wise people are able to keep their wits about them even in the face of opposition.
- Imagine drawing a line between yourself and your Antagonist.
- Climbing out of the quagmire creates a certain degree of muscle memory. Whether we're fully aware of it or not, we've been educating our heart all along about the perils that we face at the hands of our Antagonist.

Hardwired for It

- You have a knack for showing great chutzpah in the face of adversity.
- The trait of brazenness was gifted to Israel, allowing us to guard, maintain, and regain control over ourselves.
- It takes a stubborn, stiff-necked, and obstinate personality to block out your Antagonist's radically imposing agenda.

Pursuit of Wisdom

- We've been designed to develop a keen, mindful discernment, to enact good judgment, and to be shrewd in order to acquire wisdom. This helps us to maintain an unapologetic attitude.

- The words of a brazen person are toxic to some, but with proper intention, they may also be used to arouse, excite, motivate, inspire, and inflame oneself to learn and to pursue wisdom.
- Hashem's Torah is likened to a blazing inferno. To properly receive it, you have to match it. You must also be on fire!

Chapter 15: By Invitation Only

- The Antagonist first appears at your doorway as a wayfarer, then it masks itself as a guest; by the third visit, it manages to transform itself into the master of your house.
- When you suddenly find yourself in conflict with our Antagonist, and that old negative behavior or thought pattern starts knocking you around—it's because you invited it in.
- Not letting it in takes practice. Through trial and error, you become wiser to it, but in order to do that, you must first become cleverer about how we perceive it.
- Developing a wise attitude toward it demands a certain degree of grit. When it comes to solicit again, the wise person in you will be able to look to the doorway in your mind and trumpet, "Go away! I'm tired of letting you in."

Let It Be

- If you use something meant for the good in a bad way, your misdeed will follow you home. It perches itself next to the door, obsesses over you, and loiters there until you regain control over it.
- Is there a wicked wild beast that's just lurking, waiting to overpower you and drag you into its lair? On the contrary, the beast always appears to be unconcerned and is peacefully resting.
- It desires you. You've stumbled, whet its appetite, and now it craves to be with you—it's hungry for you.
- This *teshukah* depicts a kind of devotion or longing for love. It seeks to be loved and fulfilled by you.

Master It

- When we underestimate its power, it becomes master over us. We feel the pangs of emptiness, and long to be near it. It shows up at our door, and we welcome it in. We send the invitation; we invite it into ourselves.

Counterattack

- When self-doubt, anxiousness, obsessions, and blindness start to flow inward, your power of preservation awakens. A normal reaction is to get ready for the counterattack.
- Losing your whereabouts leaves you feeling vulnerable. You get stuck in a fight-or-flight. If you attack, you are just attacking yourself. It's self-harm.
- Your Antagonist may only achieve its real purpose in life when you rule over it, control it, and direct it.

It Ain't All Bad

- People are born with both good and bad natures. One is not more dominant than the other. They both begin in a state of rest.
- We begin educating children about goodness between the ages of eight and ten because eventually the badness is going to wake up.
- It's wise to beat it to the punch and take prophylactic measures by teaching them early on how to use the good while leaving the bad behind.
- The only reason our Antagonist awakens from its static, raw, and inanimate position is because we water it, feed it, nurture it: we empower it. We wake it up!

Chapter 16: Quick as a Deer

- Your heart and your mind may awaken you to action, but it's your legs that propel you toward your destination.
- Your legs are vehicles for doing good in this world.
- It's possible to leave the bad in the dust by running toward goodness.

- The path in which you wish to take, there you shall be led. Your legs vow to take you there.

Let Your Legs Do the Walking

- When you're in a sticky situation, it means that both your heart and ability to make proper decisions have already been compromised. Leveraging your power of distinction is no longer an option.
- When stuck in the Antagonist's trap, speaking to your legs is your only way to jumpstart your heart.
- Once your body is mobile, the wisdom in your heart resuscitates, and then your legs guide you back on track.

Chapter 17: Do, Then Listen

Feet First

- Actions speak louder than words (King David).
- Before you part your lips, it's best to first take a moment of silence, and your Antagonist will be tricked into thinking that you're someone else; it will read you as a wise person.
- There are times when silence trumps transparency. When you remove yourself from view, you may quiet your mind and place your thinking aside.
- Now you can reset your compass, walk to your new destination, and safely revise, rescript, and verbalize your narrative in a more positive light.

Shake a Leg

- Let your legs do the talking.
- The "do, then listen" business approach: After boldly jumping into a new position, only then do you start to learn the ropes. You pick up the basics afterward.
- You may leverage the same businesslike skill to spring yourself back into action.

- When feeling paralyzed and stuck in a seemingly never-ending negative pattern, it's often necessary to take such an extreme leap of faith.
- It lifts you off the ground, shifts your vantage point, and affords you a new perspective.
- Once you've taken a step forward, you're now in a position to guide other people to take a leap beyond the face of the unknown.

Fear of the Unknown

- Do, then listen: overcoming the fear of the unknown is a part of your legacy.

Get a Jump On

- Seeing what lies ahead with a bird's-eye view is a wise way to prepare before you head out on your journey.
- Avoid letting the Antagonist get muddled up in your actions from the get-go! It'll just weigh you down, and your nature is already very heavy.
- In order to leap forward, you have to go against your own nature. With the right amount of enthusiasm, you can give yourself the lift necessary to get a jump on life.
- Doing acts of kindness helps you to rise above your physical nature. This is just the boost you need to empower yourself to continue to stride forward.
- You're not expected to do this all on your own. You receive *chizuk* directly from Hashem.

Shpilkes

- Maintaining a low level of *shpilkes*, impatience, helps you to stride forward.
- Life is never stagnant; you're always in a state of transition. You're either moving forward or slipping back. It's in your best interests to always be moving toward greater spiritual heights.
- We bless the living "to go in *shalom*," as they move toward greater spiritual heights, transforming and perfecting themselves.

- Death is the loss of the treasure of life. That's why we mourn. We lament the loss of the opportunity to continue striding forward.

Chapter 18: Run Away

- Run away from your problems!
- In order to seek *shalom*, you must "remove yourself from bad."
- It's important to know exactly where you're headed.

Danger Zone

- The danger zone exists between one structured environment and another.
- Unless you've established your next destination from the start, you're most likely to leap straight into the danger zone.

Eyes on the Prize

- Hashem's Torah is our address, and as long as we keep it at the forefront of our minds, we'll continue to walk the straight path, and our legs will be compelled to move in the right direction.
- When you stumble, you can get back on track by reminding yourself of what's important, meaningful, and valuable in your life.
- Doing something positive, an act of kindness for another person, is the quickest route to reignite the wisdom in our heart. Once it's awakened, your eyes will be better focused on the prize.
- Hashem's mitzvos keep you on trajectory.
- Hashem accompanies you on your journey.

Nachas Ruach

- Every action you do draws down vital energy from above. This vitality helps you to do more things of the like. It doesn't sit quietly. It puts on the pressure until you're encouraged to act again.
- Whether this descending energy is good or bad, when you actually see things through, you always receive a bit of *nachas ruach* (comfort) in the end.
- Your acts of kindness invite good energy to cascade from above, inspiring you to do more positive acts for yourself and for others.

Flee from Misdeeds

- Badness works like a boomerang. One step in the direction of home and you cleverly leave that spot uninhabited. You aren't there when the boomerang returns.
- Wise people know that when a negative thought floats up into their minds, it's still within their grasp. It's still within their control.
- Your best recourse is to drop it and run.
- Running to do what may appear to be even a trivial mitzvah leaves any misdeed in the dust.

Chapter 19: Run Toward Yourself

- Hashem told Avraham to both "Go to yourself!" and "Leave yourself behind!"
- When you exit, what you're actually accomplishing is twofold. On one leg, you're uprooting yourself from your current position and leaving all of your Antagonist's negative odds and ends behind. On the other foot, you're already heading to a new address that offers you hope for a brand-new beginning.
- When you're headed out on your spiritual journey, in order to slowly peel yourself away from your familial haunts, it's helpful to review the wise steps that Hashem laid down for Avraham Avinu upon his own exit: he was first told to leave his country of origin, then his birthplace—the city he grew up in—and lastly, to step out of the door of his father's house.
- Sometimes, the closer you are to home, the more difficult it is to create a disconnect.

Wherever You Go, There You'll Be

- Before divorcing yourself from the place from which you are fleeing, it's important to have fully invested yourself in your current situation. If you haven't wholly tried, you're most likely to trip over the same challenges upon your new arrival.

Greener Pastures

- It isn't any easier being green. Beware of the grass-is-greener syndrome.
- When you're feeling deficient, down, anxious, or confused in your current situation, it's common to want to cast your eyes on the behaviors of others.
- This leads you to covet what they have, and the grass starts to look greener on their side.

Change Your Mazal

- The events that you experience in life are connected to a higher flow, which channels through the *mazalos*—the fiery spheres and stars that radiate from above.
- Hashem is your beacon.
- The great big balls of fire in the sky represent your relationship with destiny. Your relationship to your *mazal* impacts you both physically and spiritually. It has the potential to both fill your cup with wisdom and line your pockets with riches.
- You may change your *mazal* by having open dialogue with Hashem and being kind to others.
- When you walk your own path, live according to your values, and fulfill your purpose in this world, the *mazalos* release their control over you. You are placed right back into the arms of Hashem, and it is only He who guides you.

Change Your Place

- Any place to which you attach yourself becomes a receptacle for the inflow of your *mazal*.
- When you're committed to your present space and, for whatever reason distanced yourself from it, you're bound to experience a loss. When you get up to leave, your relationship to the space suffers, and you're likely to lose touch with your own whereabouts. You lose your power of distinction.

Chapter 20: Bare Bones

Keep It Simple

- We're the ones who complicate things.
- Baby steps allow us to accomplish one thing at a time. It's just not possible to take on all of our struggles at once.
- To become a wise person, we must start off wholly simple. So, be the simpleton!

Stay Relevant

- People were once more inclined to work on improving the mitzvos they were already doing.
- To make the mitzvos more vibrant, one must perform them with a little more forethought, added feelings of greater purpose, and a bit more focused attention on Hashem.
- Centralizing your energies even once a week is a wise thing to do.
- There's nothing more practical than taking something that you already do well and just trying to make it better one step at a time. All the complicated stuff falls by the wayside.

The Simple Recipe

- The matzah ingredients are simple. And simple moves. It's quick, light, and it won't slow you down.
- There's freedom in poverty and simplicity. Less is more. And too much extra can be too much of a burden. Unnecessary extras just weigh you down.
- True freedom comes with simplicity. A free person is nimble. A quick leap and the clever person becomes unstuck.
- Walk your own path by focusing your energies on making something that you're already good at just a little bit better.

Simple Therapy

- Outside-in activities, external systems, and new tools aren't always a real plus.

Less Is Better

- Instead of adding pollutants to your relationship, maintaining a simple recipe keeps it nicely crisp and fresh.

Sweat the Small Stuff

- Sweat the small stuff, not the big stuff!
- The people who achieve the most in life are the ones who are willing to be stringent with the easier stuff.
- When you treat that which you imagine to be light as if it's heavy, then that's what you put your heart and sweat into.
- Taking what you're already good at and making it a little bit better is your greatest investment.
- Putting slight pressure on what's already natural and easy for you to do allows you to grow organically. When you cultivate a small idea in this way, it eventually leads to huge results. You simply can't know what sort of gift or reward might come out of every small deed.
- This world, the *world of action*, hangs on small actions.

Less Is More

- If you're struggling in your life, try to find something you enjoy. Seek out something enriching. All it takes is to do a task that you already enjoy for about three to five minutes a day.
- It's important to stick to it even when you're not *feeling it*.
- It's important to apply your power of establishing fixed times to all of your transformational endeavors.

Cut Out Burnout

- Don't turn three minutes into an hour (or even fifteen minutes). If you do, you most likely won't find much inspiration to do even one minute the very next day; you'll have burnout.
- Your Antagonist doesn't just kick you when you're down; it also looks to mislead you in times of great inspiration. It knows that you have the capacity to get overloaded with the things in life that bring you much joy and pleasure.

- Not placing a limit on your creative flow is just asking for it to topple over. It's hard to achieve anything when your creativity is spilling everywhere.
- In order to cut out burnout, it's best to stick to your own given times and parameters.

Primary vs. Secondary

- Placing all of your energy into what's secondary doesn't just take away from what's truly important, but it also causes your creative flow to spill out. This, too, leads to burnout.
- Focusing on what's primary in your life allows you to accomplish more and makes you lighter on your feet.
- That's because you're focused on what actually deserves your center of attention. Directing your creative energies toward what's secondary just weighs you down.
- It's essential to find for yourself a confidant, a person who's willing to be your advocate. An advocate's job is to reflect back to you what's most vital in your life.

SECTION VI: WALK YOUR OWN PATH

Chapter 21: Pursuit of Peace

- First, you remove yourself from the bad, then you do some good, and then you're free to pursue *shalom*.
- Your ability to separate the bad from the good is indicative of your capacity to understand one thing from another. This is due to your power of distinction.
- When you know in your heart of hearts what's best for you, nothing should be able to impede you from running after *shalom*.
- Negativity is super sticky, and focusing on the bad will simply cause you to get more entangled into it.
- The intention is to free yourself of your Antagonist's influence, not to hurl yourself deeper into your negative thoughts and behaviors. Doing so will more likely lead you to stumble, start feeling down, fall out of touch, and lose your *whereabouts*.

- An important thing to remember about trauma is that it's cyclical and compounding. When people who have experienced serious trauma in their past end up having a traumatic day, both the initial trauma and every subsequent trauma resurfaces, leaving them with a heightened degree of psychological pain. They're stuck reliving all of their traumas in the present moment.
- Remove yourself from bad *by way of* doing good.
- Don't go it alone. It could be life-threatening.
- Sharing your negative story is an effective way to start striding forward. In addition to feeling understood, you begin to hear the damaging words that you speak, and you become more attuned to the way you've been choosing to tell your story.

Chapter 22: Creating Shalom

- In order to gain strides on your negative thoughts, behaviors, and feelings, first create *shalom* with your Antagonist.
- When writing about what's bothering you, make sure to follow the four guiding principles:

  1. Choose One!
  2. Be Practical!
  3. Start Simple!
  4. Be Relentless!

- The power of imagery is an amazing tool for helping you walk your own path. You can picture meaningful scenes in your mind and then later retrieve them. That allows you to relive those memories whenever it suits you best.
- It's the negative events in life that tend to leave the most residue. Fortunately for us, these negative images are helpful in our efforts to demarcate the boundaries of the path that we are walking.
- The retelling of a negatively charged experience brings your story alive. You're the author of your story. Telling your personal narrative allows themes to rise to the surface that are relevant for you today.

Your Antagonist Story

Here and Now

▸ It's important to recall a negatively charged story because that's how you create a *benchmark* for yourself. It's a reminder of the times when you encountered your Antagonist and things didn't really go to your liking.

▸ Being able to tap into this memory, to imagine yourself telling your story in such detail, means that it's still with you. It's not just something that happened in the past. You're still carrying it around. Your ability to describe it in the *here and now* means that it's still alive.

▸ That makes it a useful resource. You may see certain aspects in your *Antagonist Story* that are relevant to your situation today.

Benefit Theory

• If you've been carrying around this issue for a couple of weeks, a few months, or even years, you must be benefiting from it in some way. If you weren't benefiting from it, you would have dropped it a long time ago. People don't hold onto or do things that don't benefit them.

• When you become wiser to it, and you become conscious of the fact that this particular thought or behavior is no longer working for you, you're able to develop a firm attitude toward your Antagonist.

• When you start to refuse your Antagonist entrance into your circle of consciousness, that's when you know that you've placed yourself back in the driver's seat.

Twist in Perspective

▸ When we find ourselves lost and confused, we may have an inkling to relinquish ourselves from the negativity. But truth be told, we like to cling to our negative thoughts and behaviors. We actually enjoy the emotional rush that they have to offer.

> ▸ They tend to remind us that we're still a living and breathing organism. We may be actually drowning in them, but they look to be our *lifesaver*.

Your Benefit Story

- It's a real twist in perspective when you realize that it's possible you've been holding on to your greatest concerns because you might miss them, along with the benefits that they provide.

Chapter 23: Peace Treaty

Ceasefire

- The moment you can give your Antagonist a name, you can create an emotional disconnect by recognizing it for what it truly is—an entity in and of itself. This is your first step toward establishing with it a peace treaty.
- *Shalom* grants you the space and the freedom to see through its cunning schemes and exposes the deceptive role that your Antagonist has been playing in your story.
- You no longer have to let it define who you are. You can author your own story and control whatever role your Antagonist is going to play in your personal narrative for the future.
- What's bothering you is simply a useful tool to help you walk your own path.
- Establishing a ceasefire will end the conflict, and drafting an agreement that respects your need for self-determination removes the influence it has on you.

Chapter 24: Building Confidence

The Road to Confidence

- One of the secrets to walking your own path is to be conscious of the fact that you've always been on your own path and that you'll continue to be on your own path. When feeling down, anxious, or out of control, you may perceive yourself as being off track, but in truth, you haven't veered away from your path at all.

- Walking with confidence is what keeps you on track. It's an attitude. Every opportunity to pull oneself out of the muck is a confidence builder. And as you continue to live according to what you truly value, it will require a much thicker wall of deception to deter you.

- As you continue to stride forward, you encounter many beginnings.

Heading Out

- Imagine yourself unpacking the extra weight and consciously leaving behind the external messages and behaviors that have been misleading you.

About the Author

Rabbi Shimshon Meir Frankel is a clinical psychologist with over twenty-five years of experience in helping others navigate their relationships—with their families and with themselves. He has adapted his approach in order to serve clients both online and in person, as well as within the framework of the department of family and social services in the local municipality. With his special blend of *mussar, chassidus,* and *machshavah,* Rabbi Frankel utilizes a soul-brewed, person-centered, Torah-driven approach to therapy, assisting people to discover their purpose and find value and meaning in their relationships.

Rabbi Frankel lives in Zichron Yaakov, Israel, with his wife and children. He can be contacted at shimshonmeir@gmail.com.